mirco wolf wiegert

fritz and goliath

the story of fritz-kola

mirco wolf wiegert

fritz

and

goliath

how to build a successful business
from scratch

Econ

Econ is part of the
Ullstein Buchverlage GmbH Group.

ISBN: 978-3-430-21073-7

Translated from German by: Ben Kamis
Editing and proofreading: Fortuna Communication
Book jacket & flipbook layout: Rocket & Wink, Hamburg.
Interior layout: Tanja Pfaff, Hamburg
Set from the Tasman
Typesetting: Eberl & Koesel Studio, Altusried-Krugzell
Printing and binding: GGP Media GmbH, Pößneck
Printed in Germany

for all those
who are and have been awake
with fritz.

► ► ►

▶ ▶ ▶

foreword

"Good morning Mirco, you'll find a short itinerary for next Friday attached. (Yann has planned a route that we can manage just fine on foot.)

See you next Friday!

Yann & Jannis"

I'm sitting in the train from Hamburg to Berlin. I'm still wearing an FFP2 face mask, but the sun is shining outside, the vaccination program is making progress, and the end of the COVID-19 pandemic seems to be in sight. A day with Yann & Jannis awaits me in Berlin. These two "fritzes" make sure that fritz-kola is available in all of Berlin's pretty places. All the little cafés, bars, restaurants, rooftop patios, parks, clubs, riverside promenades; all the places people are soon to gather after months of lockdown. All the places where an ice-cold fritz-kola or another one of our soft drinks or juice spritzers would sweeten the moment as we enjoy others' company. We're going to do our part to enable everyone in the hospitality industry and their guests to enjoy this special moment in the post-COVID era.

I remember as if it were yesterday how I drove from Hamburg to Berlin in my old VW van to bring the first fritz-kola into this throbbing global city. It was still the infancy of fritz-kola. We didn't have any employees yet, no money, and little experience of what it's like to be a "good entrepreneur." But we had an exciting journey ahead of us that we were to travel with many great people. They're mostly guys and girls in their twenties, enthusiastic to get involved with us. Over the years, more veterans have joined to enrich our enthusiasm with experience. Today, just before the copy deadline when this book goes to press, fritz-kola has grown up, become adult. With nearly 300 fritzes working in Germany, Belgium, the Netherlands, Luxembourg, Poland, and Austria, we sell fritz-kola in virtually all European countries and operate five bottling plants at capacity.

Although most of this book is written from my perspective, fritz-kola is and always has been more than the story of "the two faces" on the bottle — Lorenz and me. fritz has encountered many people over the years: the caffeine expert in sales; the server in the bar; musicians who survived their tours with our help; the bottling machine operator working through summer nights to fill orders; the fan thrilled to see fritz in un-expected places; the hater annoyed at our communication

and stances … We've encountered countless people. Some of them will have their say in this book.

My tale is not just about our corporate history, but also about my experiences, crises, and eureka moments as an entrepreneur. Those planning a startup and budding founders can perhaps draw inspiration from it for their own projects or find encouragement to walk their own paths. The most important thing is to start walking.

We live in an age of social change. I would like to communicate respectfully with my book and provide all readers with an easy read, regardless of gender or heritage. Therefore, I have opted against gendered language in general cases, naming individual women and men in specific cases to be fair to all and give them their due. The terms "fritz" and "fritzes" are fundamentally gender neutral and simply refer to the great people who work for fritz-kola.

Mirco Wolf Wiegert
Hamburg, May 2021

prologue

"Lorenz, it can't go on like this! We need to get the word out!" I was nervous. We had had some initial success with fritz-kola, and it looked like our business might work. But publicizing our product by going door to door from one pub to the next was unbelievably tedious.

"We need PR! A real coup!" I argued, as we walked along Schulterblatt St. in the Schanzenviertel district of Hamburg one afternoon. We were carrying a crate of fritz-kola between us — we were on our way to pitch at a new bar. "But how can we reach a bunch of people at once? We don't have any money for advertising! And no contacts in the press either!"

Back then in 2003, the internet sort of existed, with AOL and stuff, but the world of being able to spread an idea over Facebook, Twitter, Instagram, and YouTube rapidly and virtually for free was still far away. But then something happened to really get the ball rolling.

"We have to get together with people who know about publici …" "Hold the crate!," Lorenz interrupted me and sprinted across the street. Unlike me, he wasn't one to hesitate. He was a go-getter — a self-assured, cool guy. So he jumped directly in front of a Smart car that was just

prologue

pulling out and knocked on the driver-side window. The car bore the logo of the *Hamburger Morgenpost*, a tabloid popular among students at the time. The *MoPo* had had its reporters-on-wheels zipping through town in these Smart cars for some time. And Lorenz tried to convince the *MoPo* guy that driving away would cost him a really great scoop.

The reporter's curiosity was piqued: Matthias Onken, not much older than we were, then visited the two of us in my dorm room on the west side of Hamburg. We immediately put a bottle of fritz-kola in his hand. As he casually opened the bottle with his cigarette lighter, he gave himself a hickey when the ballistic bottle cap ricocheted hard off his neck. He wasn't expecting it to be so fizzy. He took it with humor — along with a crate for the news office. The next day he approached students in front of the University of Hamburg. The young women and men on campus were to test and evaluate our kola. A few days later, a two-page story appeared about the two students who were taking on Coca-Cola, the global corporation. We had hit the jackpot. The fritz-kola story was gaining momentum.

To be perfectly honest, back then I never could have imagined the entrepreneurial success story that these two were about to write.

matthias onken, then *mopo* reporter

Student life was really pretty great. That was especially true for me because I had completed my vocational training as a forwarding agent before going to college, so I knew how much freedom I enjoyed as a student, unlike many others who had enrolled straight after graduating high school. There was more autonomy in my life than I ever could have dreamed of as a nine-to-fiver.

I could decide for myself whether, when, and how intensively I was going to pursue my studies. I didn't have to be grinding or at the loading ramp at seven a. m. following orders. And I could drift through the bars until late became early. Of course, so much responsibility comes with a catch: it requires a lot of self-discipline. Those who aren't made for it will eventually get stuck as perpetual students, bouncing from one McJob to the next because the career path isn't mapped out. It's up to each individual to decide what they want to do later and to take the appropriate steps.

My best friend Lorenz and I were in that phase in 2002. We were studying, working part time, and asking ourselves what was to come after our final exams. After my experience with vocational training, I knew that I wanted to be my own boss, and I dreamed of being an independent entrepreneur. That was fairly uncommon at the time. Most of our classmates were aiming for a job at a big company. There was no startup culture like there is now. At the turn of the millennium, the economy was in bad shape — there was a recession, and the shock of 9/11 was still fresh. The new economy of publicly traded tech firms had just collapsed, and the unemployment rate was high relative to today. It was hard for college graduates to find a good job.

Moreover, the tendency some people have of shutting down ideas with phrases like "that'll never work" was even more widespread then. People who believe in their own abilities and visions are quicker to try self-employment nowadays. But back then our compulsion to stand on our own two feet — or at least to give it a try — made us complete oddities. We simply weren't interested in hearing our bosses' and coworkers' two cents about our work. Instead, we just wanted to see how self-employment might work and how far we could get with it. So it was time to get a business license, build a working office, write some invoices, create a product, and sell. And finally, to earn some money with it.

But how does one run a company anyway? At least I had deliberately chosen my majors to suit my career dream of becoming an entrepreneur: foreign trade and international management — business stuff. And like all other business students in my year, as a freshman I

participated in the classic "pizza project," in which we learned the ABCs of entrepreneurship — especially the famous four Ps of price, product, promotion, and placement — by founding a virtual pizzeria. We hadn't yet realized that other subjects were still to come, including market analysis, purchasing, bookkeeping, staffing, leadership, capital, and later, debt management and so on. Maybe that was for the best. I was just really stoked to see the 4P pizza project through from fiction to reality, and it had to be together with Lorenz. We were simply curious about how to run a company. We hadn't yet given any thought to how we were supposed to combine such a playful small business with our studies, our jobs, and our personal lives. We also took it slowly, just occasionally meeting without much discipline for a year before the actual founding. But some decisions in life take time to ripen, even if it's impossible to say later what one actually did during this "ripening stage."

In fact, we didn't determine what our business was going to consist of at all until quite late. We had an idea book, a dog-eared pad of foolscap, in which we scribbled down any notion that occurred to us. Then we developed and elaborated them a bit. That's how we came on the idea of a bocadillo shop — a kind of bar where we would sell great sandwiches and great coffee. We brought that idea back from Spain during a train tour through Europe we had taken together in 1998. At the time, the idea was relatively new in Germany, Starbucks having just recently opened its first locations here.

Another idea in the hospitality field was to open a hostel. We also considered a cleaning crew or a handyman service. Customers could simply call us, and we'd come and clean up or fix things for cheap. Our focus was on products and services that students would use or want to have.

One thing was certain: we were after something concrete, not strictly virtual. Besides that, we were looking for an occupation that would be fun and that we could do together. The idea of developing a new kola, one that was better than the others and even better than the market leader — stronger, richer, more awake, less sweet, no plastic, only glass bottles — occurred to us over a frozen pizza and a cola in the kitchen. The target market: students and people who like to go out. And it was to be a kola, not a cola. It's just one letter, but even today it remains a symbol for everything we wanted to do differently.

The idea intoxicated us, because the advantages of this product were immediately clear to us both. Cola can be made to order as well as stored, and it keeps for quite a

while. It can be sold to corporate customers (B2B) and consumers (B2C) alike, and they consume it, so it gets replenished. It's also something people consume daily, and it costs very little compared to a luxury good. Producing individual batches doesn't require much capital because everything that involves expensive machines and plant can be outsourced and performed by others. We didn't even need a storefront or anything; a cheap warehouse and a few square meters of office space would do. But the principal argument in favor of the kola was that this product promised the most fun for the 7,000 euros (about $8,300 U.S. dollars) that we could scrape together. And because kola is just a cool product. And because it would let us continue to be active in the scene we liked: cafés, clubs, bars, and pubs. And because there was money to be made!

Even then, most people associated "startup" with computers and software. But that wouldn't have been nearly as much fun, even if it would have made more money. Of course, we were interested in more than just fun. We understood that founding an enterprise was going to be a lot of work, but we were both ready for it.

That fritz-kola would be so successful or work so well was not at all part of the plan at the time nor even within the limits of our imagination. We just told ourselves that we were simply going to start making a kola and see what happened. Good or bad, mistakes or not ... who cares! The first thing was just to get started and see whether we could really make any money. If it didn't work, we could stop at any time, learn from our mistakes, and try one of our other business ideas. We wanted to combine work, fun, and independence. It was more of a side project than a plan for world domination, but it involved real money and real people.

By the way, I continue to make note of new insights, ideas, and inspirations even today. Maintaining these collections of ideas is an exercise for myself. And it's a lot of fun to sketch an idea out quickly and develop it later. Unfortunately, "Volume 1" of our idea book with our kola idea went missing during one of the company's moves. I've seen that happen in many companies: in later years it's easy to be casual about the documents from the founding era. A sense of the preciousness of such "evidence" and the effort to archive corporate traditions comes only later, not during the turbulent growth stage. Before disposing of your first folders with those early sketches, the business license, and maybe even a hand-written, amateurish business plan, my advice to all founders is to cram them under your bed or store them in your parents' attic. You'll be happy to have them later,

to be able to flip through them and show them to others. At least I still have my first, very own crate of fritz-kola from those initial, turbulent days.

from idea to ingredients

For quite a while, we had nothing more than a vague plan: we're making a kola. First and foremost, we were pretty normal young people who would rather fool around and party instead of diligently and systematically pursuing a project. College, girlfriends, and jobs took their toll. After all, we had to make a living. But it soon became clear to us that we wanted to run our company full time as soon as possible. At first, it was a side gig by necessity.

Looking back, I consider it an advantage that sheer lack of money forced us to take one step at a time, without immediately setting up offices, staff, and so on. As a result, we knew every aspect of our business because, for several years, we were dealing with them all ourselves on a daily basis. In the beginning, we knew each of our customers personally, and we could reanalyze the market situation every day. It would have even been dangerous had a rich uncle paved the way for us financially from the beginning. With lots of money, you can get into lots of mischief. Modest financial means necessitate greater diligence and more thorough deliberation. At fritz-kola, we always made the biggest mistakes when we had enough cash on hand.

Founding on a part-time basis was the right approach for us, and it can work for others too because earning a living with a regular job helps a person stay grounded. But determining the right strategy for a startup naturally depends on the product. Someone going after a new market, like Amazon, where all that matters is which monopolist comes out on top, has to let it rip from the get-go and come to terms with the fact that the business won't turn a profit for several years. Similarly, someone with fantastic prospects — perhaps through a lucrative licensing deal — can go full tilt right from the beginning and take out a loan. But anyone entering an existing market as a small newcomer, as we did back then, should be immediately profitable, grow step by step, and remain flexible in order to constantly identify niches in the market. Besides that, I wouldn't have grown as much had I started with an annual salary of 50,000 euros and just delegated everything. We were just doing our thing independently, and paying for that freedom with long hours and an initially very modest standard of living was perfectly fine. It never seemed like a lack to us that a

new car, extravagant vacations, or starting a family at a young age were out of the question. We were doing exactly what we most wanted to do. Building a business with maximal commitment and simultaneously enjoying a maximal standard of living just isn't possible.

Sometime around the end of 2002, it became clear to us that it was time to progress from idea to ingredients. We imagined that it would be so simple: first we would search for lists of ingredients and recipes on the internet, buy what we need in the supermarket or — if need be — the pharmacy, and then somehow mix them together into a kola until we liked the taste. The idea was something like this: mix one cinnamon stick and a touch of vanilla; grind a few crumbs of cardamon and cloves in a mortar; add a few squeezes of bergamot and lemon; season with some freshly pressed ginger, a big spoonful of caffeine from coffee, and a scoop of sugar; top it off with caramel syrup for a nice black color; add water and carbonation; stir and we're done. But that plan quickly proved to be naïve. We couldn't put it into practice until many years later when in 2021, we launched our new fritz-kola organic kola.

In 2002 we didn't yet know how to make a beverage out of these ingredients. Figuring out how to produce caramel coloring, which is sugar that is caramelized and then liquified, without it tasting burnt is no easy task either. So it never came to the point of us actually stirring anything. We quickly realized that we would never produce a kola that way. I know now, by the way, how to brew an excellent classic kola or a genuine organic kola. The latter is a little easier because organic recipes get by with fewer ingredients. We now have experienced staff at fritz-kola, women as well as men, who go into great detail.

Back then it was obvious that we needed professional help, someone who would produce the kola according to our specifications. We started looking up the addresses of breweries and mineral water producers, and we became one with the telephone. "Hello, my name is Mirco Wiegert. Can you invent a new kola recipe for us? And then make a few crates of it?" We heard everything from roaring laughter to awkward silence. It was really rough going, and it was a good exercise in an important virtue for all entrepreneurs: patience in the face of frustration. As a founder, you sometimes have to bang your head against the wall for days on end, but that's the foundation for later success. After over 40 rejections and plenty of muddling through without giving up, we finally got lucky in late 2002 when we found a small brewery in Weser-bergland. "Boys, you're clueless," said the master brewer with a mix of congeniality and pity. "But sure, I can help

you. Just tell me exactly what you want and we'll make something decent out of it." Jackpot!

We knew one thing for sure: there was no point in trying to taste like the leading brand because people could already buy their product. Our kola was to have a distinct kola flavor and plenty of caffeine, but taste less sweet and more lemony — a little more adult. At the end of the day, we wanted a kola whose flavor we enjoyed and that made a cool impression. That is often a good criterion in product development: would I use it or consume it myself? Would I like to give or receive it as a gift? It's easier to intoxicate others and carry your enthusiasm out into the world if you're already a fan of your own high-quality product.

Fortunately, the master brewer was also hooked, and he tapped his network for us. Many cola and soft drink recipes are devised by experts trained in that art who work for beverage-industry distributors. They draw the basic flavors from extracts of raw ingredients and make them into a syrup. The syrup is then mixed with water, carbonic acid, and sugar in decentralized bottling plants, where the final product is packaged and finished. Once the master brewer called and told us that the process was complete, we went to see him, and he presented us with two different kola varieties to try. We liked both, so we

asked him to produce a small amount of each and to bottle them in plain, brown beer bottles with contrasting caps. Being able to distinguish recipe A with the white caps from recipe B with the green caps allowed us to postpone the decision. We placed a small order for 170 crates of both varieties and returned happily to Hamburg.

Could we have imitated the flavor of a Coca-Cola? Maybe. Despite the fact that all the good recipes are kept under lock and key, any formula can be replicated with a little time and expertise. Even if the original recipe is stored in a highly guarded safe in Atlanta, what really matters is whether anyone could notice the difference between the original and an imitation. At the end of the day, people buy a beverage, and it just tastes how it tastes. Who's really going to do an A/B test to detect the nuances? Doesn't this one taste a tiny bit different from that one? If the flavor meets the consumer's expectations, then it's all good. How many milligrams it contains of exactly which ingredient is an afterthought.

It was important to us to have a distinctive, more mature flavor. The new kola was supposed to give people a real caffeine buzz, much stronger than Coca-Cola. Our kola was supposed to help people get through long nights. We wanted it to have a real kick to keep people alert for a few hours, for it to work, for it to wake people up and keep them awake — just the ticket to make it through a long study session, to prepare a project, or to party. Therefore, we added the then maximum legally permitted dose of caffeine in kolas: 25 milligrams (mg) per 100 milliliters (ml). (For comparison, Coca-Cola contains about 10 mg.). We intend our slogan, "lots-n-lots of caffeine," to be taken literally.

That's why fritz-kola, like Coca-Cola and all other colas, are not appropriate for children. We add caffeine by the shovel! As a psychoactive substance, caffeine is something for adults, and it doesn't belong in children's bodies. Accordingly, we have never produced advertising aimed at children or adolescents.

In my view, a cola without caffeine is pointless. You want that kick. Cola drinkers don't just want a sugary soft drink; they're looking for that caffeine buzz. While energy drinks may contain more caffeine, they also expect people to tolerate the taste of gummy bears, taurine, and overly sweetened fruit.

The glass bottle was a priority from the beginning. No plastic. But to be honest, it wasn't initially about ecology or sustainability. Like everyone, we too had to learn to be environmentally conscious. With the glass bottle, we were focused strictly on the pure enjoyment of kola.

We knew from experience that, when you come home exhausted after a hard day, and you want to reward yourself with an ice-cold cola, the form of the refreshment makes a huge difference. Either you pour a glass of cola from a plastic bottle (which might not even fit in the refrigerator and from which plenty of the carbonation has already dissipated), drink it straight from the plastic bottle (which somehow always seems lukewarm), or you grab a small, ice-cold glass bottle and enjoy the fresh, cool kola. That's the only way to really treat yourself, to give yourself a little reward. It definitely tastes different when drunk from a little glass bottle than out of a plastic bottle or a tumbler. Lots-n-lots better.

This message, by the way, is also present in Coca-Cola advertising: the man in a t-shirt, quenching his thirst on a hot day, naturally drinks from a little single-serving glass bottle, not from some 1.5-liter monstrosity or an old pickle jar out of his mom's cupboard.

Right. Back to the glass bottles. Nowadays, they're sleek little numbers made of clear glass. And the little bottles found in bars are our own creation. It goes without saying, however, that back then we had to make use of commonly available bottles. The first product test went with the brown beer bottles mentioned before. They looked conspicuously like prototypes, without the classically cool appearance one expects from a kola. To show that the bottles contained kola rather than beer, we opted for white beer bottles from the second shipment onward. We and our test subjects found that they made the right impression for a scenester drink. They emphasized fritz-kola's style as a drink for parties and bars. And they stood out. In truth, we also had a purely pragmatic reason for choosing beer bottles: it was all the brewery supplying us could fill.

from product to brand

By this time, we knew what we wanted to produce, what flavor and effect it was supposed to have, and how we would bottle it. But the baby still needed a name and a suitable visual style. Looking back, I can tell that our gut instincts guided us well in that decision, which certainly contributed to our rapid success and the brand's positive image. I'd love to be able to say that we had the strategy all planned out at the time ... Of course, we wanted to build a relevant brand, and we also knew what "relevant" meant to us. What in hindsight might look like a stroke of genius by two college students, though, was in fact the product of necessity.

Let's start with the name. It has definitely played a part in our success. Had we tried to sell the same product under the name "Harbor Water," we certainly wouldn't be where we are today. And the converse is also true: a completely different product — given the right quality — would have found success using the name "fritz" in its marketing. "fritz" — it sounds a little cheeky, like the *Klein-Fritzchen* character who pops up in jokes, akin to Little Johnny. It sounds uber-German, perhaps even vaguely northern German, and it communicates the product's origin immediately. Many languages use "Fritz" to refer to any generic German. Fortunately, "German" is no longer automatically associated with the "Thousand Year Reich." German products are now more typically known for Made-in-Germany quality standards. From our particular vantage point in the club and restaurant scene, the worldwide hype about Berlin also communicates a positive image of Germany and generally helps to sell a brand with German roots in other markets.

We had a whole list of potential names at the time; there must have been thirty of them. Unfortunately, the list has gone missing. But most of the ideas emphasized our core sense of Hamburg and northern Germany in a fairly conventional fashion: "Alster Kola," "Elbe Kola," "Northern Kola," "Hamburg Kola," or something of the like. The epiphany of "fritz" was an outlier in the results of our brainstorming. It was our favorite, and although we didn't want to rely on our opinion alone, we lacked the money for professional market research. Therefore, we planted ourselves in front of a mall on Hamburger St. for a few hours and asked passersby which name on the list best suited a kola from Hamburg. "fritz" was the favorite by a huge margin. That settled the name. In my view, the process of finding the name is a great example of how a lack of money unleashed our creativity. We had to figure it out ourselves. With the support of a rich uncle, we would have probably hired three different agencies to come up with the name, paid 20,000 euros for the exercise, and it's unlikely that any of them would have landed on "fritz." It's important for a company to go through the process of figuring itself out, as long as the discussion doesn't continue for its own sake and go around in circles, which would be more of a hindrance. But it's generally an instructive process, including the mistakes made along the way.

We had been working on the brand's visual image simultaneously. Usually, just developing a logo in cooperation with a specialist design agency would cost far more than we had in total for our little startup. To save money, we had decided to go with a monochrome

logo because printing the labels in black and white would be cheaper than if they were in color. As for the motif, we opted for a picture of ourselves, which saved us the cost of licensing images. We simply stood in front of a blank white wall in the ping pong room in our dorm's basement and took a snapshot with an old-school camera before bringing the film to be developed at Budni, a chain of drugstores in Hamburg. But at least the prints were on a digital CD. We then somehow shifted the pictures around at home on our computer using a version of Microsoft Word that can now only be found in museums, and we made a monochrome silhouette graphic out it. With the graphic in hand, we went to a neighbor of ours in the dorm and asked her to make our jagged silhouette a little more appealing. And that's the story of fritz-kola's enduring trademark: a black-and-white silhouette of two students' heads.

We had yet to land on our branded lettering. I spent two weekends experimenting at home and cobbling together bitmap graphics until we finally had the basis for our own new font and lettering. That saved us the licensing fees for proprietary typography. It was a strictly low-budget operation. We opted against capitalization because the miniscule letters struck us as hip and modern. And it suited our common aversion to dealing with complicated orthography. <mark>Now it was time to find out how people would actually react to our kola.</mark> We dressed up the white and green-capped bottles that the brewery had delivered with the labels of our own design. We printed a bunch of labels in a copy shop and pasted them onto the bottles with a glue stick.

The field test was our moment of truth. In late 2002 we threw a party in the Kellerbar — a bar in the basement of the *Emil-Wolff-Haus* dormitory where I lived in the Othmarschen district of Hamburg. We sold highballs containing a mix of our kola and rum from the discount supermarket. Our dormmates and guests were simply to vote on which kola they preferred. We kept a tally behind the bar. Everyone knew that we were using them as guinea pigs and that we had had the kola made specially for this purpose, but they were really into the idea. What they didn't know, however, was how much caffeine it contained. Everyone was surprised to find themselves partying until ten a. m. The stuff worked as advertised, tasted great, and had people partying all night. The winning recipe — the kola with the white cap — scored a decisive victory. I'm not sure whether all those tipsy people could and really did differentiate the white caps from the green ones, but who cares? A decision is a decision, so we placed the first real order: 240 crates of

24 clear beer bottles each, filled with kola and loaded onto six pallets.

Since we didn't have the money to have the order shipped to Hamburg by truck, we cruised down in the old VW van and a way-too-big trailer to pick up the crates ourselves. That January 30 officially inaugurated fritz-kola's production. We watched our kola being mixed in a big tank, and it was a crazy feeling. This very simple process — first dissolving granulated sugar in a tank before adding water, syrup, and the extracts — was being done on a fairly primitive, small scale, but it was all we needed at first. And due to our lack of a warehouse, we spread our inventory among the basements and garages of our relatives for quite a while. The first order lasted until April, at which point we did have to reorder.

The official birth of our business also happened without any pomp, fuss, or celebration. On February 28, 2003, we simply showed up at the Hamburg Chamber of Commerce on Adolphsplatz behind the city hall and registered "Hampl & Wiegert" as an unlimited private company. It cost us 28 euros apiece. That was it. Nobody asked for a business plan or anything. Contrary to popular belief, it's super easy to register a business in Germany. The bureaucracy might get out of hand sometimes, but its thoroughness makes up for the slow pace. With our registration, we automatically became (compulsory) members of the chamber of commerce, but it wasn't too painful because the dues are determined according to revenue. We were also registered with the tax bureau and received a tax number, so we were ready to really get rolling.

I had already registered the logo and lettering as trademarks with the trademark office in Munich a few months prior. The trademark registration is still available on the internet, showing the day of November 11 and just how cockeyed and homemade the logo and lettering originally looked. Over the years, we've polished their appearance a little and tweaked the lettering a bit, but only those with trained eyes and those who know what to look for would notice it.

The registration for fritz-kola was filed with the trademark office on February 11, 2003, and it was valid for ten years, so it had to be renewed in December 2012. Beyond that, we took out some business liability insurance so that we wouldn't be plunged into debt if we damaged other, fancier cars while out delivering our product or something. That covered the formal stuff.

We felt that we had done everything necessary to get started. We've since been repeatedly asked whether we didn't have some kind of business plan with revenue

projections and whatnot, whether we had given any thought to our branding strategy, how we were going to tell our story and stuff. Sure, we did. We had a whole loose-leaf page. Unfortunately, the original plan has since been lost, but it hasn't been forgotten. It looked something like this (seriously!):

business plan:

we're not going to borrow any money.

the product:	kola with lots-n-lots of caffeine, less sweet, and only in glass bottles
the team:	lorenz and me
target market:	college students and everyone who hangs around the schanze and st. pauli districts
price:	in the ballpark of coca-cola
distribution:	via hospitality businesses (cafés, bars, clubs), doing the deliveries ourselves at first
advertising:	none (ideas and money)
competition:	coca-cola
total address-able market:	infinite
organization:	the two of us will do everything for now except bookkeeping (we'll hire an accounting office for that)
office space:	unnecessary
storage:	in our relatives' basements and garages
financial model:	rough product calculation: how much can we pay for a bottle of fritz-kola, what other costs are involved, and what's left over for us if we sell the kola for a price of x?
our stake:	7000 €, a vw golf, a vw van, two computers and printers, plus lots-n-lots of elbow grease.

That was our business plan. A good book on the topic had been recommended to us at a startup initiative, and we were well aware that one sheet of loose-leaf paper was a little thin. Before attempting an epic plan, we first wanted to gain some experience and gather some real numbers. I sometimes gasp when I think back on how little we knew then about producing soft drinks, about the market, about marketing strategies, and so on …

lost in the desert: the soft drink market in the early 2000s

Thinking back, it's hard to believe how pathetic the range of non-alcoholic beverages was at the turn of the millennium.

coca? cola? kola?

The term *cola* derives from a medicinal syrup that an American pharmacist, John Pemberton, blended in 1885 using the highly caffeinated cola nut. By contrast, the term *coca* derives from coca wine, which itself was a variation on *Vin Mariani*: a Bordeaux *à la coca du Pérou*, indicating that it contained real Peruvian cocaine. It provided an energy rush, invigorated the imagination, and suppressed hunger. Today, it would probably be considered a party drug. Pemberton's rapidly popular and sought-after energy drink contained cocaine until 1903, which is the origin of the brand name *Coca-Cola*. It would, however, be misleading to call the currently leading brand "the original," as there were numerous colas available in the United States at the time.

When it came to cola and soft drinks in 2002, Germany resembled a socialist planned economy: you could only get the bare necessities. Most restaurants offered a garden variety mineral water, Coca-Cola (occasionally Pepsi), orange Fanta, Sprite, and apple juice. For kids, there was *Spezi* — cola mixed with orange soda. What can I say? It's a German thing. Any establishment offering orange juice or even tomato juice counted as a very classy joint. And sometimes you'd see — hold on to your hats! — *Kiba*, which is a mix of cherry and banana juice. That was it. Cola was generally served as an open beverage poured into a glass from a plastic 1-liter bottle.

How could any customers or restaurateurs live with such monotony!? There had to be room for something better!

When we invented our brand in 2002, we naturally wanted to distinguish ourselves as clearly as possible from the monopolist and thus opted to spell *cola* with a *k*. What we didn't know at the time, but only happily learned later, is that in Spanish (the practically non-existent) *k* is often used in deliberately rebellious misspellings. For example, *casa ocupada*, referring to a squatter house, is often (mis)spelled as *kasa okupada*. We couldn't have come up with a better reason for our *k*. fritz-kola should wake people up, so we're happy for *our k* to disturb people's reading habits. By the way, our spelling also alludes to the German spelling of the original and eponymous *Kolanuss* (cola nut), although most modern colas no longer contain that ingredient. The desired quantity of caffeine is now added directly in pure form. At fritz, we use natural caffeine derived from coffee.

Even without the new varieties of soft drink that we offer today, maybe at least more than one kind of cola? To discover a niche as entrepreneurs, we simply reflected on what annoyed us as consumers — where did we see room for improvement? Of course, it was also important for the product as well as the packaging to be cool. There is far more flair in holding a *cool* bottle — in every sense of the word — than in holding a glass of lukewarm cola. The more modern word for it would be "Instagrammable": presenting a product or setting so attractively that a picture of it would go viral on social media and look good on a phone's display. But even long before Instagram, it was clear that we had tapped into the *zeitgeist*. Many restaurateurs appreciated that we were offering them an alternative. The beer industry was already paving the way with stylish bottles and brands like Becks, Astra, Tannenzäpfle, and Corona.

It was obvious that we were taking on a real Goliath. At the time, Coca-Cola was the archetype of a global brand. Its status wasn't restricted to the beverage market. Asked to name a global conglomerate at the time, no one would have answered Amazon, Google, or Apple, but many would have come up with Coca-Cola. By comparison, we were just two college students who wanted to launch a new kola.

Paradoxically though, the existence of that top dog made it easier for us to attract the attention we needed and to get people interested in fritz-kola. Restaurateurs and retailers were used to competition in liquors, beer, and cigarettes, but there were virtually no competitors for cola and soft drinks at the time. As a result of their unchallenged monopoly, the folks at Coca-Cola had grown complacent when it came to service. They didn't have to hustle for placement on menus and in retail stores because nobody could afford not to sell Coca-Cola. By contrast restaurateurs were used to being swept off their feet and spoiled as customers by breweries, distilleries, and cigarette brands (which we did not, in fact, know at the time). The soft drink field, though, was being completely neglected.

It was a completely new experience for the restaurateurs and barkeepers to have us stop by personally and behave with normal congeniality. We had no idea how Coca-Cola worked in terms of service and customer relationship management, so our approach certainly wasn't a clever strategy. We were just keen to stop by the bars ourselves. More to the point, we didn't have any other distribution channels. Still, the market leader's overconfidence was definitely to our advantage.

In hindsight, it was also a boon that Coca-Cola was in

the middle of a restructuring process at the time, and they were mostly preoccupied with themselves. In that kind of situation, even a tiny newcomer to the market can shoot past on the outside lane and just keep cruising until they suddenly pass the finish line. At the time, we couldn't have known what was happening over at Coca-Cola, but we suspected that we were so small in their eyes that we would stay under their radar. We kept our focus on ourselves and our own goals, and we were fortunate that our optimistic gut instincts paid off, and fair winds were at our back in the beginning.

broke and booming

To found a startup, you need capital. That includes space,
production plant, staff, and the money to pay for it all.
We had practically nothing. We did have some building
savings contracts that were included in the capital-
accumulation benefits from our apprenticeship days,
and we liquidated them. Counting everything that we
could scrape together, our startup capital consisted of a
whopping 7,000 euros and a small pool of "fleet vehicles":
Lorenz was making payments on a used VW Golf that he
had bought — which was a great little car — and I was
driving an old VW van. That was it.

Many founders would take on outside capital in that kind of situation. In our case, we wouldn't have had much chance beyond our parents and other relatives. Crowdfunding didn't yet exist, and who else would have wanted to invest in us? We wanted to keep our plans under wraps until we had achieved something, so asking our relatives for a loan was out of the question anyway. And I wouldn't bet a cent that they would have actually lent us anything. At any rate, I wouldn't have taken it personally if they had refused in light of our casual naïveté in the early days.

That a bank would extend a loan to a couple of college students with negligible collateral and the harebrained idea to have a go at Coca-Cola — the global market leader — was even less likely. But we didn't care. We didn't want to take on any debt, not from anybody. It would have meant dependence, and that's exactly what we were trying to escape in the long term. Independence was one of the goals we had set for ourselves, which is why we resolved at first to only spend money that we actually had on hand. We didn't want to be in hock to anyone, so we tried to operate according to the motto of "creativity beats capital." Looking back, I think that lacking capital was a blessing in disguise because it forced us to focus and not to start too many things at once. In later years, when we were more successful and more financially liquid, we made some mistakes simply because we could. The company was stable and could withstand some blows. Entrepreneurial types with pronounced egos are especially prone to letting too much money seduce them into making poorly considered or outsized decisions.

One consequence of our extremely thin capitalization was that we operated for the first few years as an unlimited private company. That's not the usual way to incorporate a beverage company because the owners personally bear unlimited liability, and they'll be paying off their creditors forever if they run the company into the ground. An LLC, where the liability is limited to the company's assets and excludes the owners' property, would have been a more sensible choice. But for that we would have had to shell out 12,500 euros in share capital with another 12,500 euros in reserve. We simply didn't have it. It wasn't until five years later on March 1, 2008, that we rectified it and continued on as "fritz-kola GmbH" — a limited liability company.

It took about three years before the two of us could live off fritz. Until then, we had to keep regular jobs on the side. Lorenz worked at a TV production company, and I temped in the bookkeeping department of an eyewear chain. Everything we earned went toward our living

expenses; we had nothing left over to subsidize the company. At the same time, we kept our college classes going on the back burner. For several years, we had no time for hobbies, sports, or anything like that.

We didn't initially have any offices, so we managed the company on the go: in cafés, bars, and at the kitchen table in my dorm. It also took a while to arrange a warehouse. As set out in the business plan, we continued to store the crates in my grandparents' downstairs utility room in Norderstedt and in Lorenz's parents' basement. We also lugged them in and out by ourselves because we didn't have any staff yet.

Producing the first real batch of 240 crates of 24 bottles each practically exhausted our startup capital. But if everything from that point on went according to plan, there would be hardly any further costs beyond gas. If, however, one of our cars had broken down at that stage, we would have faced some tight times. But since the first batch got us on the right track, we were able to pay later operating expenses out of our income. Our gross margin on each crate of fritz-kola that we sold was only enough to buy one or two cups of coffee in a café, so we were operating from hand to mouth for a long time. Our policy of accepting only cash on delivery, but paying only at the last minute of the payment deadline to preserve our scant liquidity, didn't help much. Later, when beverage dealers picked the goods up directly from our warehouse, we issued invoices to them immediately, and we sometimes managed to deduct the funds before they had even unloaded the crates from their trucks. That was the only way for us to maintain our cash flow without having to take out an operating line, which we wanted to avoid if at all possible because of the cost and the dependence.

Problems with liquidity are a common "cause of death" for young, undercapitalized companies. I have the impression that some founders underestimate the importance of a steady, healthy cash flow. Invoices don't go out until long after the service is performed, and then if the client misses the payment deadline, they're too slow to follow up. On the other hand, they don't take care to negotiate payment terms with distant deadlines to give themselves as much time as possible before having to pay. Such practices show neglect for the vital importance of internal financing, which can spare a company the expense and dependence that come with outside capital. Founders in particular should pay close attention to their financing, even in times of low interest rates. It has served me well to monitor the income and expenditure on a daily basis and to track them assiduously. That's how we've managed to avoid liquidity issues. On occasions

when our balance was perhaps a little too thin to pay large bills on time (which happened only twice), we called our creditors and told them that we'd like to pay a little later. Putting your head in the sand when problems arise is never the right option. Unless you take action, things will almost always get worse, never better. As it turned out, delaying the payment was no big deal. Most suppliers are understanding and grateful when their clients reach out to inform them promptly and on their own initiative.

It's also important for founders to ensure a healthy margin right from the beginning. If a business model cuts it too close, a single unforeseen expense, like a mechanical breakdown or a defaulted invoice, can blow a hole in the balance sheet that could prove very hard to fill. That goes double if outside capital is at stake. In this respect, founders must be brutally honest with themselves when considering whether the business idea can really work, whether the enterprise will be able to stay afloat and keep those mouths fed. Before getting into the early years of fritz-kola, let's rewind a bit: what kind of guy was that who partnered up with his best friend to cause a little trouble in the soft-drink market?

where I come
from

My father always loved a challenge. One sentence he often repeated was "C'mon, let's get busy!" "Busy" is, of course, the root of "business."

mirco wolf wiegert

What kind of person is determined to become an entrepreneur? There are as many stories as there are people
who feel the need to go out on their own. Here's mine.

When I was born in 1975, my father was self-employed
as a merchant at the local market. But I grew up mostly
with my single-parent mother. She worked as a secretary,
and we had a very modest standard of living. It wasn't
much of a problem for me, though. Where I lived, the
used look, which is another way of saying hand-
me-downs, was generally considered hip. "Fast fashion"
had yet to appear in the 1980s. The division of society
into rich and poor was not as pronounced as it is today.
The neoliberal reconfiguration of the world into one
where everything is measured in monetary value and
kids are judged by their richer classmates based on the
logos they have (or don't have) on their clothes was just
getting started. My mother managed to save enough for
us to go on proper, regular vacations, which hardly any
single parent can achieve nowadays because the
distribution of wealth is becoming ever more unjust.

The Boy Scouts also had something to do with the fact
that money has never played a major role in my life.
Once my friend Lars (now a restaurateur in Hamburg)
brought me along to one of the troop meetings, they
became my second home. I later met Lorenz there — I

was eleven and he was nine. We quickly became best friends. I also met most of my other friends there. The Boy Scouts were a moneyless society — other things beyond mere material possessions mattered more, things like solidarity, endurance, and the willingness to take responsibility for others. Status was a question of poise and character, and it couldn't be bought with brand-name sneakers or other trappings of wealth. Another reason that experience made such a profound impact on me was that we would be on the move together for weeks at a time, and we'd stay up all night around the campfire.

The Chernobyl nuclear reactor disaster occurred on April 26, 1986 — toward the beginning of my Boy Scout days. It caused schoolyards to be closed and travel plans to be postponed or canceled. We children noticed that the adults were extremely shocked and apprehensive, and that the world had changed all at once. For quite a while, fresh milk, fruit, and vegetables were scarce. Schoolyards and playgrounds were closed for weeks. Back then, the hoarding favorites were milk powder and canned milk. When the COVID crisis dominated public life for months starting in March 2020, I was reminded of some of those restrictions.

The nuclear meltdown also made it clear to me that we mustn't take the natural environment for granted —

preserving it takes effort. A love of nature was another product of my time with the Boy Scouts. Growing up in urban Hamburg, the trips throughout Germany and Europe revealed to me the peace and beauty of untouched landscapes. We hiked, went canoeing and rafting, and we traveled across the continent on overnight trains.

But I also saw how appalling pollution and environmental degradation can be. That includes rivers that are too polluted to bathe in (which was the case with the Elbe in Hamburg at the time) as well as the carelessly dropped glass bottles littering the forests. Even today, seeing the detritus of the industrial world out in nature drives me crazy. The passion I share with fritz-kola for reusable packaging originated then.

I inherited my entrepreneurial spirit from my father. He started out selling stuffed animals and other gift articles at local markets before expanding into outerwear, shoes, and gift articles sold from his own stores. While I was still young, he taught me to appreciate independence, entrepreneurship, and hard work. When I think of him talking about a successful project, it's as if I can still see his eyes light up before me. And I still clearly remember the eureka moment when he explained to me the importance of the difference between the purchase price and the sale price, which I understood immediately. I was six years old.

My first conscious memory is from even earlier. I must be three or four years old, and I go to my father in the kitchen very early in the morning. It's still dark outside. My father is eating breakfast and getting ready to head out to the market. His fervor and enthusiasm for his work at such an early, early hour impressed and influenced me greatly. How he went out and did his thing. When I was staying with him and he had to work, he'd simply take me with him. Once, we drove out together to a market outside of Hamburg, and we spent the night in his stall. I found it tremendously exciting — an adventure.

It was completely normal at the time for kids to watch over their parents' shoulders as they earned a living and to help them out. I think it's still a good idea for kids to lend a hand and to literally grasp how their parents feed the family. Later, I helped to renovate his stores by setting up new shelves and whatnot. It went without question. Experiencing my father's business reinforced my determination to be my own boss and to be independent — and I think it has also affected my sense of responsibility toward my staff.

In spite of it all, I have made mistakes for which I'm

still ashamed and for which I've apologized to those affected. I used to have a short temper. I would shout and slam doors when things didn't go as I had planned. Then there was the time Lorenz and I developed a handbook on internal procedures, projected it onto the wall, and had employees read it out loud. How inappropriate. We were founders at a garage startup, and we didn't know the first thing about leadership. We were unprepared because we didn't know any better at the time.

After the dorm party in 2003, when we revealed to our families that we had started a business, my father was skeptical at first. I could read the unspoken question from his facial expression: "Do you think you can manage that?" But it didn't discourage me. On the contrary, the doubt in my father's eyes was another source of motivation. I still suspect that many successful entre-preneurs are driven by the desire to refute the skeptics who doubted them — fathers, mothers, teachers, former bosses ... The skeptics love to come back later and say things like, "He wouldn't have amounted to anything if I hadn't been so hard on him." But in doing so, they're grossly overestimating the role they play and retroactively mistaking their lack of support for a master stroke of motivation. If a founder's only impetus is to refute someone, the venture isn't likely to amount to much.

It would lead them to take unreasonable risks, to waste energy, and to make foolhardy decisions precisely because someone had warned them. But to be clear: my father has always given me practical support when necessary, and he's as thrilled about my accomplishments as I am. Thanks, dad, for lending me that big trailer for the van, and sorry for driving it into the ditch on those icy roads.

I might not have become an entrepreneur had I listened to my paternal grandmother. She didn't directly criticize my father's trade, but she did like to make broad generalizations about the merchant's way of life. For her, selling something to someone was no different from conning them into the purchase. She didn't consider it to be honest work, which might reflect her upbringing on a large farm. My great-grandfather once ran the old family farm near Salzgitter before taking on a big farm in the Altmark region and expanding it into a bigger agricultural operation. He sold to cooperatives, so he never had to actively market his produce. The end of the war was also the end of the farm, and my great-grandparents came to West Germany, where their children took them in.

One thing I definitely learned from the situation at home was to be careful with money. It started with my

allowance, which amounted to fifty pfennigs (less than one dollar) a week in elementary school. My beloved *Yps* comics cost a deutschemark (or "D-mark") and a half. It wasn't always enough — even though my father and grandparents would occasionally spot me an extra D-mark. I learned then never to waste money and not to aspire for the things that money can buy. But thanks to all the time I spent with the Boy Scouts, that wasn't too hard.

Dealing with my mother is where I learned how to bargain — like many kids back then it was usually about television. It was strictly regulated at our place. I was allowed to watch *Sesame Street* from 6:00 – 6:30 p.m., and that was it. Sometimes I'd be allowed to watch the odd Saturday evening show. But I had to bargain hard for the *Muppet Show*, which was on Wednesdays. Similar ideas about child rearing were behind my childhood cola ban. First, it was too expensive and, second, it was considered unhealthy. Perhaps the fritz-kola story truly began in our parents' cola-free kitchens …

It's always good for a laugh when I speak at corporate events and I'm supposed to talk about my school days. I can calculate and deal with numbers as a business-man now, but for some reason I was a complete dunce in math at school. It's something I really had to work on later in college and since — how to deal with Excel spreadsheets and stuff.

My strengths lay more in politics and history, which always helped to balance out my grades. Our teacher of politics in history was the biggest influence on me. It was impossible to tell where he stood politically, which earned my respect even then. He took a pass on the perfect opportunity to influence us students toward his way of thinking because it was more important to him that we learned to come to our own conclusions.
I liked that. And it always drove me to rebel if someone acted as if there were no alternative to their own opinion. I never liked it when opinions were expressed without justification and questioning them was discouraged, especially on the part of institutions. When it came to topics like macroeconomics and the principles of investment, my college leaned neoliberal, as was then fashionable. That perspective ignored the environmental effects of boundless economic growth and preached the retreat of the state from virtually every area. I liked to question this market-oriented ideology, which was sold to us as objective science, even if I lacked the detailed knowledge to do so. One professor called me the "King of the Counterargument." It didn't bother me that my objections relegated me to

a minority position and I sometimes had to take heat for it.

I worked in outpatient senior care for the period of my compulsory civil service. As a side project with my Scout troop, some parents, and members of the Boy Scouts organization, I converted the unused attic of a local community center into a Boy Scout clubhouse. I'm still satisfied with how I spent my compulsory service rather than joining the army, as many of my friends did, which at the time mostly meant getting plastered and counting down the months.

After finishing my civil service, I first completed the vocational training course to become a forwarding agent. My parents told me to "learn a trade, do something practical," and that's how I wound up as a trainee at the Hellmann Brothers shipping company in the Wilhelmsburg district of Hamburg. I really am very grateful for the two-and-a-half years of good, thorough job training. Still, my independent father's passion for entrepreneurship kindled my own, and soon I wanted to start doing my own thing. So how could I prepare myself to pursue that goal even better? I registered for a degree in Foreign Trade and International Management at the Hamburg University of Applied Sciences. To pass the time before classes were to begin, I worked various jobs,

including as a vehicle inspector for a parcel delivery service. My unenviable task was to point out flaws in the appearance of the vehicles to the "independent contractors" driving them, which they perceived as a form of bullying and with good reason. I also worked several jobs as a student.

When looking for a job, doing something interesting and learning something new were more important criteria than how much the job paid. Among others, I was a salesperson for a bakery, I worked for a private property management company, and I played tour guide on bus tours around the city. Working at Instant Sleep, a backpacker hostel in the Schanze district, was really exciting. Hosteling was something totally new at the

time, and we were the first one in town. It was like a youth hostel for adults, but less stuffy and with nicer décor. I had become acquainted with hostels, their low prices, and contact-hungry clientele during my prior travels, and I was absolutely determined to work in one. So I applied at Instant Sleep, and I was hired as a cleaner. After a few weeks of cleaning rooms and toilets, there was an opening for a night clerk, and I finally got the exciting job at the front desk.

People sometimes ask me whether attending college and getting the degree prepared me for the actual entrepreneurial work that followed. On the one hand, it did because many of our instructors were experienced practitioners from the business world. I learned a lot from them. However, the subjects of team leadership and responsibility were unheard of then, which was a severe oversight. Dealing with the people in a company and leadership skills are the most important subjects for an entrepreneur, as I have since learned. People alone make enterprises — everything else is secondary. But when we started fritz-kola, hiring staff was out of the question. We were really getting started, but at first we did (almost) everything on our own.

the first step is . . .
awesome

Most of us were young, we identified deeply with our jobs and the company, and we were happy to be part of it. The danger was that we'd lose ourselves in our work and start living just for fritz.

patrick keller, sales and marketing 2008 – 2012

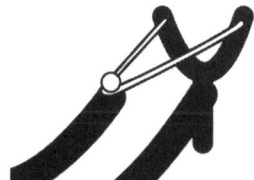

When we founded the company, Lorenz and I resolved to maintain a sharp separation between the business and our private lives. Our girlfriends knew that we were up to something, but we didn't involve them. The same applied to our friends and families. We wanted to pull the business off, just the two of us, and we developed tunnel vision. The advantage was that nobody could meddle with our plans or disparage our ideas (nor could they hop on our bandwagon and take advantage of us), but there were also disadvantages. We were in our own bubble. We weren't part of the scene we were producing the kola for, nor did we network with other founders. The courses, support, and networking opportunities offered by chambers of commerce and business groups were pretty thin, and they were too old-fashioned for us anyway. We attended maybe one or two of those meetings, but we were bored out of our skulls because they consisted simply of old men boasting about how they accomplished the postwar economic miracle back in the stone age. The opportunities currently available for founders, like coworking spaces, networking meetings, mentoring programs, or even something like angel investors didn't yet exist — probably because there were far fewer young founders.

Fortunately, the culture and attitudes have changed:

being an entrepreneur is cooler than it used to be, it has a more positive image, and many are very open and transparent about their ideas and visions. Had Lorenz and I been sitting in a coworking space rather than in the dorm, we would have quickly realized the value of sharing, and that people will only show you things if you're willing to show them something too. I encourage all founders to use every opportunity to network and share their experiences. And if there are no established networking opportunities in your location or industry, then take the initiative and start your own network!

A columnist for the *taz*, an alternative daily newspaper, visited us not long after the founding in 2003, and the resulting piece referred to us as *Stinos* — a slang term for "squares." The fact that we had no idea what the word meant did serve to prove the author's point. We were completely ordinary, at the opposite end of the spectrum from hip and cool. We didn't care much about appearances. For example, I wore my parka pretty much everywhere, just like a Boy Scout would.

We didn't come clean to our friends and family until we had invited our dormmates to the kola party. Their heads shaking in disbelief came as no surprise to us. When I told my family about our business, which was already well under way, they needed a little while to

understand what I was up to. And then everyone predicted that it was doomed to fail. "You guys are just setting yourselves up for a fall. It'll never work. Coca-Cola is way too big." That's exactly why Lorenz and I had kept it a secret for as long as possible. We knew what was coming. But as soon as we needed to use our parents' and grandparents' basements and garages as storage space, we had to own up to it. After they got over the initial shock, our families supported us admirably. I can still remember how my granny bought us a dolly cart and later a pallet jack because she could no longer bear to watch as we lugged the crates from the car to the front door and then down into the cellar.

And what did we tell the first restaurateurs we met? What did we tell anyone? Today, it would be called a "pitch," and we spent a long time perfecting our spiel. Back then, we'd simply head out, talk to whomever was behind the bar, and ask for a fresh glass with ice to serve them a perfectly chilled sample. We would introduce ourselves during this process and explain what we were up to: a local kola from Hamburg with more caffeine, only in glass bottles and no plastic. It simply fascinated some people. They thought it was off the wall — a new kola, garnished with a couple of weirdos. And they deliver it personally to boot! It's low risk, they said to themselves, so let's give it a go. A few of them did give us the impression that they were agreeing to take a crate out of sheer pity. But who could blame them? Two young guys stroll in with a crate and want to sell cola in beer bottles? It probably seemed pretty naïve, especially in light of the one dominant company in the market that also sold cola. At first, we wanted to minimize the risk for the cafés and barkeepers, so we offered everyone to buy the product back, no questions asked, if they lost interest in fritz-kola. But we only had to do so twice. We were quite happy with that failure rate, since we were enjoying so much success elsewhere.

That was how we convinced our very first customer, Gerrit Lerch, who had founded and was successfully running the Bedford and bp1 joints on Schulterblatt St. with Marc Pagel, to add us as an alternative kola in their establishments and soon to offer our brand exclusively. None of the guests complained, but his staff practically revolted against the decision. They were of the opinion that the only way to make mixed drinks was with Coca-Cola. That bias persisted in the scene for quite a while. I managed to dispel the concerns of Gerrit's people by joining them for a staff meeting and explaining a few things about fritz-kola to the 15 or so attendees. I also let them decide for themselves by pouring them

rum and cokes and whiskey and cokes using fritz. After a trial period, the ice was broken. We've managed to repeat this pattern ever since — we can always counter and overcome initial doubts.

the gloriabar

The Gloriabar in the Eimsbüttel district of Hamburg was a forerunner in cooperating with us. Falco Wambold opened the bar in 1997 and runs it to this day. That corner of what is now a trendy area was seriously run down when he started, and the same was true of the neighborhood pub that he took over. With little capital, a lot of work, and even more style, he renovated the place and has since turned it into a first-rate destination. The furnishings are timelessly stylish, with many homemade details, like the wall coverings that are made of assorted pieces of old furniture.

Falco describes our first meeting in 2003 in his own words:

An old VW van stopped in front of my bar, and a thin, inconspicuous young man walked into the bar with a bottle in his hand. He was selling a new kola and asked whether I'd like to try some. We quickly developed a rapport, and we both knew what we wanted. Mirco was still very new to the business, but he had a clear vision of how his product would fare on the market and under what conditions. The idea of challenging the monopoly with a local kola conceived in Hamburg made immediate sense to me. The slim selection of non-alcoholic beverages at the time was one reason; the political situation was another. My customers and I were on the same wavelength — due to the war raging in Iraq at the time, we weren't thrilled about the American lifestyle and were open to new things. I remain convinced that the anti-American sentiment at the time was an important factor in fritz-kola's breakout success.

On the spur of the moment during my first meeting with Mirco, I insisted on an exclusive Gloria label as a precondition for us to try fritz-kola, and Mirco agreed right away. That would be unthinkable today, but it's important to remember that fritz-kola was just a nonentity at the time; they weren't even in training pants, they were still in diapers. Acquiring some initial customers, like the Gloriabar, was therefore important for the new kola to thrive in the market.

It was the same story with Bionade — I was one of their first customers too. And I'm a star among bar owners. I make brands. Mirco and Lorenz were just two college kids out to try something. It was as simple as that. And that's why fritz continued delivering me and my team our own custom

"Gloria-kola" for nearly two years. Eventually, the logistics of stopping the machines for a few of my Gloria bottles became too impractical, which I could understand. By that time, the exclusive kola idea had served its purpose for both of us.

Thankfully, I offered their kola exclusively from the beginning. My guests went for it immediately and enthusiastically. They felt that this having this kola exclusively in "their" bar somehow also made it theirs. The same went for my team, who enthusiastically supported it. I think that the appealing image of the new kola was more important than the taste, but if my guests hadn't liked the taste, I would have quickly stopped the experiment.

For the first year, Mirco would always deliver the crates himself, lug them down into the cellar and take the empties away. A beverage distributor later took over that task, and I ordered from them too. But Mirco and I remain close — we became friends, he'd read to my kids, we'd often meet at parties or on our own, that sort of thing. When times were tight, we'd even split the odd hotel room while attending trade shows.

I've always seen and respected Mirco as an ambitious entrepreneur, as someone who counts every penny, and who would rather come across as a little stingy than as some extravagant big shot. He's also willing to ask for advice and to

accept criticism, even if he sticks to his own decision in the end. He doesn't get offended if someone sees things differently and contradicts him. He's definitely a passionate entrepreneur.

I think that our friendship is part of the reason why I've remained loyal to fritz-kola over the years. Otherwise, I probably would have tried out the competition, like maybe Premium-Cola. Of course, fritz's image as "the underdog" on the market is no longer entirely accurate. That's an area where fritz needs to write the next chapter of the story as the new mainstream. But I think it's great that they engage clearly in political campaigns, like the 2017 G20 summit, and that they communicate a clear stance on social issues.

The story of Gloriabar is — with the exception of the friendship and the custom labels — typical of how customer acquisitions went: we'd drive around and hit all the cool spots one by one. How else were complete rookies like us supposed to make contact with the people who were going to serve our drink? We went door to door and literally sold out of the trunk of our car. In fact, it was exactly how my granny had always imagined traveling salesmen. It was unconventional and tedious, but it proved to be the right way in the end.

always close to the customer

We conquered the refrigerators of cafés, bars, restaurants, and clubs with exhaustingly meticulous work. Every single one individually. We'd talk to the bartenders, meet the owners, introduce them to fritz-kola and let them try it. Later, we pursued the same strategy in the supermarkets. We started with outlets of the Spar chain and expanded into the Edeka outlets. First, we'd speak to the people in the beverage department, and then we'd make the deliveries personally. Every single store. We had soon attracted enough attention that independent retailers like the Niemerszein/Wiem family wanted our kola for the Spar stores that they owned at the time, long before we achieved our big breakthrough.

Many beverage producers don't deliver their products themselves and have no contact with the locations where their product is sold. Distributors do it for them, and they also manage the flows of product and money between the producers and the consumers. New beverage producers will turn up at the distributors seeking to have their product listed, that is, included in the distributors' selections. The decision depends on more than just taste, niche, or a cool image. The distributors usually expect listing fees, warehousing fees, and so on as compensation

for their services, like warehousing and customer acquisition. We chose a different route. By selling directly to the hospitality industry and supermarkets, we proved to the beverage distributors that our product would sell, and it wouldn't clog their warehouses collecting dust. We first stoked our customers' demand. When the first few restaurateurs started to ask their beverage distributors for fritz-kola, it was often the first time the distributors had heard of us because they hadn't listed us yet.

There were far more beverage wholesalers around the turn of the millennium than there are today, and many of them specialized in a particular market segment, like supplying the hospitality industry. The KGB beverage distributors operating in Berlin, Bremen, and Hamburg are one example. They originally grew out of the squatting scene in the 1980s before establishing themselves as suppliers for the hospitality industry. *KGB* stands for *Kollektiver-Getränke-Betrieb* (the Collective Beverage Company), though some say it also stands for *Kohle-Gips-Bier* (Coal-Gypsum-Beer) beverage distribution. Michael Totke's Glasshütte 85 in Hamburg's Karo district and Ebeloe Beverages, located at the time in Elmsbüttel, came from the same milieu. The latter also supplied the Gloriabar around the corner. These beverage distributors saw small, unknown brands like ours as a chance to distinguish themselves from the competition. They became our first partners on the supplier side of beverage distribution.

Little by little, about a year after the founding, beverage wholesalers started approaching us. Many were excited about having an alternative to Big Cola, and they'd invite us over for coffee and enthusiastically list our fritz-kola. Others had a less refined conversational style: "Who are you? We'd be happy to list you. What'll you pay us for it?" Distributors of that stripe would get novices to pay extra for each step. We were completely green, and we were hardly prepared to handle these listing negotiations. We had our loose-leaf price list, our sample bottles, and our enthusiasm for our product, but that was it. It's easy to get taken to the cleaners that way.

But in fact, our disarming naïveté was probably more of an advantage. We knew that we weren't dealing from a position of strength as a "mini-kola," and we had no interest in haggling over points with industry veterans. Therefore, we decided without further ado not to pay commissions or to give any special discounts to anyone. If we treated all beverage distributors equally, we'd spare ourselves the undignified horse trading. They would either take it … or leave it. Our position was basically:

"Your customers want fritz-kola? And you want to supply them? We'll be happy to sell it to you. You will pick it up at our place. But we're not paying any extra fees, and we don't give discounts. Period." The approach of treating everyone equally, not paying any special fees, not accepting any requests for volume discounts, and extending the same conditions to all beverage distributors paid off for us. Sure, the distributors would protest at the top of their lungs and didn't hold back their criticism, but later, while shooting the breeze after the third beer, they'd usually admit that it was exactly the right strategy. In any event, we had established a client base that was already buying fritz-kola or seriously interested in starting.

We were able to gradually wind down the practice of making our own deliveries. Beverage wholesalers were soon picking up entire pallets and even truckloads of kola from our warehouse and selling it by the crate to their customers in the hospitality and retail industries. At an industry association meeting many years later, the owner of a beverage distributor took us aside and congratulated us on seeing it through to the end that way.

I strongly recommend to all founders: generate demand for your product yourself. If you do your job so well that your customers really want what you're selling, it'll be much easier going with distributors. With the economical and effective social-media communication channels, it's easier now than it was then. It didn't go viral when we converted one restaurateur; we had to start all over again with the next one. Our road was tough, and it demanded a lot of perseverance on our part. At the beginning twenty meetings would yield perhaps one order. But that's just how it goes at the start, and you can't let it get you down. Fortunately, we were absolutely committed to our kola, and we didn't let ourselves get discouraged. We wanted to succeed no matter what, and we were confident that we could solidify fritz-kola's position in the market because it was good and the market was ready. And we liked the idea of overcoming obstacles and breaking barriers. We might not go about it in so extreme and exalted a fashion as someone like Elon Musk, but the skepticism we often encountered was more motivating than discouraging.

It was also motivational when restaurateurs who had given us a try reordered very quickly. That gave us something to work with, financially and mentally. If positive feedback is still lacking despite many attempts, it's not necessarily time to give up, but it is time to seriously take stock. Sugarcoating the situation or the numbers won't help anyone. What's causing it? Is the

product okay? Is the price right? Is the promotion working? Am I looking for customers in the right place? Am I the right person to pitch this product? Do I know anyone who'll tell me the truth? Are my product and I even relevant to anyone anyway?

We, of all people, needed to learn how it goes: too much carbonation, too little carbonation, too expensive, too cheap, bottles too big, bottles too small … meeting the restaurateurs, chewing the fat, and pitching and selling the kola. We went to the first meeting together. We grabbed a crate of kola and ran down to the then most popular bar on Schulterblatt St.: the aforementioned Bedford Café owned by Gerrit. We showed him our kola, and he said "Good God, what are you guys doing with that drink?" But he got a kick out of it and bought our crate of kola for about 20 euros.

Gerrit still recalls how we'd chat up restaurateurs in front of or inside their establishments, without an appointment or any prior communication. And that we were about as cool as our cars, which is to say

not very cool in the sense of the trendy Schanze style of the early 2000s. More college-y. Somewhere between business majors, psych majors, and kindergarten teachers. Strikingly nice and driven by an insane passion for their homemade kola. Definitely confident in their product, a flair for sales, gifted in persuasion, and determined to succeed in the niche they claimed to have found. We immediately had a really friendly vibe. The weirdest thing about them was that they were totally serious about the whole thing …

There's a certain nostalgia that still connects me to fritz-kola. And respect for all that these two kids built out of nothing. It's been a real ascent and a great story. And it also pleases me somehow to think that we played a tiny part in it.

At the time, we naturally sensed a bit of skepticism on Gerrit's part. Call it a prudent business sense. Completely normal. So we gave him the chance to back out and return the goods along with our mobile number written on a waiter's pad, because we didn't have business cards yet. It didn't take long though before he called us. Our kola had been selling surprisingly well, and he wanted more, starting with another five or six 24-bottle crates. That was the very first sign that we were on to something.

After the meeting with Gerrit, we split up. Lorenz hit the nightspots, and I took on the daytime businesses. And then we went everywhere a person can hang out in Hamburg: Schulterblatt St., the Grindel and university districts, the Hamburger Berg area, Hans-Albers-Platz square, and Wohlwill St., which were the areas popular at the time for going out. When we found new customers, it was really easy for them to reorder — they could just

text or email us. And we'd come as soon as possible with a delivery, even in the middle of the night. We accepted cash on delivery. It was pretty wild how we were traipsing through dancing and dining rooms at all hours of the day and night with our kola crates.

One of our first customers was the Kleine Pause diner, run by Sabine and Thorsten Clorius, near the FC St. Pauli soccer stadium. Thorsten still recalls how our bottles weren't uniformly filled to the same level — a typical teething trouble for a newly launched product. His guests took to fritz-kola immediately, and nothing has changed. We still have a very pleasant business relationship. Whenever Thorsten needs anything, he calls me directly, even though the relationship isn't as close as it was in the beginning, because there sadly just aren't enough hours in the day. I initially handled all the customer relationship management myself, as Thorsten recalls:

When we renovated our place in September 2003, Mirco came in the middle of the night before the reopening, around one a.m., and set up the fridge that he supplied himself. Mirco also showed a lot of involvement in the following years, like when we'd participate in the block party held in front of the Kleine Pause.

Generally speaking, Lorenz and I handled the relationships with and deliveries to our initial customers, who quickly became friends, for quite a while — even long after we had enough money and staff to delegate it. But we felt connected to those people, and we didn't want to lose contact with the market out there. Another thing fritz-kola meant to us from the beginning: direct contact with our customers, lugging crates included. We didn't want to lose that feeling from the early days. Making an appearance from time to time where the real business takes place and the money is made helps all entrepreneurs who want to keep both feet securely grounded. Even now, I regularly squeeze some time out of my calendar to get out there where the action is and to gather feedback from people on the outside. I feel that this urge is indispensable. If all you see is what's happening on the inside, it's easy to be fooled into thinking that a company's internal processes are the most crucial thing. But they're just a means to the company's true end, which is to provide customers with optimal service and to generate revenue. I too should really be talking far more to people outside of our fritz orbit.

Of course, I also ran across some peculiar customers while pounding the pavement in those first years. One time, I found a note on my desk saying that I should demo fritz-kola at the Graf Salon. A hairdresser? There I stood, shortly thereafter, curious and clueless before a door in

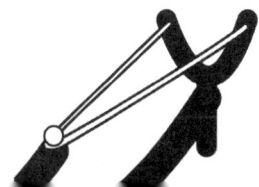

the St. Georg district of Hamburg. A very scantily clad woman opened the door and greeted me, saying "Ah, you must be from fritz-kola. We've been expecting you. Come in." I had, in fact, landed in a brothel. At the bar, I met Mr. Graf, the owner, along with my counterparts from Jägermeister. So I pulled out my bottle, gave my spiel, and told them about fritz-kola … when a bell suddenly rang. The Jägermeister salesman smiled because he already knew the deal and told me what to do. We ran down the hall toward a mirrored wall, hid behind it, and waited until the john had made his selection and disappeared into one of the rooms. And then I could proceed with my sales pitch.

Another time I was supposed to drive out into the lowlands of northern Germany. At the time, I was responsible for northern Germany in addition to the daytime restaurants in Hamburg. Deep in the country, at the edge of some woods, I came across a huge mansion behind the screen of an impenetrable wooden fence. I rang the bell, as instructed, and the door was opened by a woman who looked like a German geisha. The "master" was awaiting me, and he would be with me in a moment. There I was, back in the sex industry. The manager was dressed like a vampire, wearing all black leather with horns on his bald head. He proudly showed me his club, which included everything from St. Andrew's crosses for tying people up and flogging them and human-sized hamster wheels to replica throne rooms and dark corners for every purpose imaginable. I gave my spiel again, told him about fritz-kola, and got him in touch with the next beverage distributor to arrange reliable deliveries. I don't recall whether these customers ever became fritz-kola regulars, but I do remember being impressed at how my startup enterprise was introducing me to some places well off the beaten path.

Once I was on a sales trip to the island of Sylt. I didn't know my way around, and the location for the meeting was listed as "Buhne 16, on the beach in Kampen." I parked the car on the street, unloaded the sample crate, and started trudging the long way through the dunes. Lugging more than 20 pounds of drinks through loose sand under a blazing sun felt like a draining trek through the desert. The boardwalk to this exclusive beach bar didn't exist yet, and I hadn't yet clued in that Buhne 16 was the hottest destination around. Completely exhausted and drenched in sweat, but enjoying the beautiful ambience of the North Sea, I finally reached Tim and Sven, who ran the place. They had a great laugh and told me that they could have picked me up from the street with their vehicle … but then I would have missed

out on this unique hike through the dunes. I had no idea at the time that people would approach me with stories about their fritz-kola moment at Buhne 16 for years afterward.

Over the years of selling fritz-kola on the road, I became acquainted with the diverse restaurant scenes in northern Germany and our neighboring countries. I collected my share of speeding tickets and radar photos in the VW van and later, in the Golf. My favorite one shows me sick as a dog and wearing a hat and scarf, but the mountain of "founder dope" — Dayquil, Aspirin Plus C, a thermos of hot tea, and some Kleenex — remained fortunately out of sight on the passenger seat. I learned a lot that way. For example, I learned that the fuel gauge in a VW will always warn you soon enough, which sleeping positions are the most comfortable in a car, and how to tell a decent hotel from a dive (which required careful observation in the days before TripAdvisor and Yelp) — if a hotel's parking lot is empty, then just keep driving and searching until a more heavily frequented hotel appears. And then you can try to get the last bed.

We had come up with a price structure before our first sales meetings. There was to be one price for beverage distributors (regardless of volume, and the only deduction would be for authorizing payment via direct debit) and one price for hospitality businesses and grocery stores. No discounts for anybody. Our knowledge of the market had improved in the first six months, and we realized that we were a little too expensive, so we came down a bit. And then only in 2018 — 15 years after we founded the company — did we raise prices for the first time. Until then, we didn't see any need to change the price structure. It worked and ran smoothly, so everything was copacetic.

Never change a running system!

We conceived the price structure from the customer's perspective: how much can a restaurant pay and still make money? And then we calculated an approximate margin for the distributor, which we had originally been able to reinvest in our business as long as we had been lugging the crates ourselves. And that's how we came up with our sales price. We talked with bar owners, beverage distributors, and independent retailers to determine each factor in the calculation, and then we calculated backwards. The difference between the production cost and our sales price would be our margin. We fiddled with the price a bit in the first few weeks, but then it was all settled.

We didn't pay much attention to the competition. There was Coca-Cola, but there always would be. It didn't

matter to us in the slightest what they were doing. They were the market leader anyway. And then there was Afri-Cola and Pepsi, and Bionade was on the outside track but closing fast. There were strong regional variations at the time in Pepsi's market relevance. It was hard to find in Hamburg. Pepsi did indeed have very good advertising at one time. Their "Pepsi — The Choice of a New Generation" campaign with Michael Jackson, the most popular entertainer in the world at that time, is legendary. But the public perception of Pepsi attributes more significance to the company than it really deserves. Perhaps that's because people love showdowns, like the Beatles vs. the Stones, Bayern Munich vs. Borussia Dortmund, and — of course — Coke vs. Pepsi. The challenger is often perceived to be almost as big as the champ. We could only dream of achieving the recognition enjoyed by a challenger like Pepsi.

the breakthrough

We started to grasp that fritz-kola had a real shot when we received the first reorders. But we were still far too unknown, a brand for connoisseurs rather than a kola with a large following. Hitting watering holes door to door wasn't going to let us scale as fast as we had dared to imagine. And that's when the legendary encounter with Matthias Onken, the editor of *the Hamburger Morgenpost*, happened in April 2003.

Matthias remembers our first meeting like this:

I was in my early thirties at the time, and I'd been working as a journalist for about eight years. Back then, I was working the police beat at the MoPo — not that Lorenz's leap in front of my Smart car was dramatic enough to be included in the crime section. I can't remember precisely how it happened really. In any case, I was running around Hamburg doing research, when Mirco and Lorenz started chatting me up in their direct, spur-of-the-moment way. I visited them a few days later in the college dorm where Mirco lived and where they had worked so hard on their fritz idea. Mirco was the softy of this odd couple, like the super nice boy next door, maybe a little spacey. Lorenz came across as more forthright, not as soft and sensitive as Mirco. To be perfectly honest, I wouldn't have bet a cent that a huge success was brewing at the time. But I found the combination of a brilliant product with two relatively inconspicuous hustlers interesting from a journalistic point of view. Without the least hesitation or inhibition, they told me about how they developed their kola, about the taste-test party, and the running gag of how they mixed the first batches in a bathtub. I was a little flabbergasted when they asked me

in all seriousness what a newspaper write-up would cost.
They didn't know that you can't just buy a newspaper article
— nor that they didn't even need to. I was already taken in by
the whole fritz story; it all sounded so easy and uncompli-
cated. That's how to identify the best business ideas: they
make immediate sense, even though you'd never have come
up with them on your own. And the product these two guys
were making was simply cool. At the time, fritz was the very
first David to take on the global enterprise. All the hype in the
soft drink field didn't start until years later.

It was immediately clear to me that we, as a Hamburg
newspaper then popular among students, had to report on
this startup. And fritz will always be the kola from the college
dorm for me. I ride by on my bike almost every day on my way
into the office. I often think of Mirco, Lorenz, and the kola
from the made-up bathtub. Sometimes I get choked up
thinking back on that wild time full of freedom, but usually
I just have to grin.

A few days after Matthias visited us in the dorm and
we knew that he wanted to write something about us,
we had to go back down to our brewery in North
Rhine-Westphalia to make a pickup. So we rented a cargo
truck, which we could drive without any extra tests
thanks to our old-school 1990s driving licenses, to pick up
the pallets. On our way back to Hamburg, with our truck

full of fresh fritz-kola, we pulled into the first gas station. We wanted to see whether the *Morgenpost* had written anything about us yet. Yes, they had. And how! There was an announcement on the front page as well as a huge report with pictures on pages seven and eight. This two-page write-up in the *MoPo* was our breakthrough. We realized that right away. That's when we knew that we could be on to something really big.

At an early stage, every founder should consider the following: How are people going to hear about my product or service and that it's practically made to fill their needs? And what channels will let me reach my target audience most effectively? It's unrealistic to expect that enough people will discover you on their own, and classic, paid advertising is tricky for a low-cost product like a kola and a young enterprise with a tiny advertising budget. For billboards and print ads to earn more money than they cost, they have to generate additional sales of many more units. That can only work once a brand has

penetrated the market deeply and is widely available.
It's a vicious circle for newcomers like we two were,
especially since we had resolved only to spend money that
we had already earned.

Once the *MoPo* recognized that we had a good story to
tell, we had hit the jackpot. More potential customers
were starting to approach us, and we had a great tagline
throughout the city: "As seen in the *MoPo*."

Things have changed. Anyone who hasn't yet figured
out how to use their phone for publicity by attracting
attention over social media has lost the game before the
kickoff. It's a constant, piecemeal process. Analog media,
ones with a reach comparable to what the *MoPo* had, no
longer exist. But I don't need to tell today's founders how
to attract attention and gain traction with social media.
The digital natives are better at it than I am anyway.

In every startup legend, there's the garage, the place
where a couple of yet-unknown geniuses cobble
something together or come up with a big idea. There
were times when we would have been happy to have a
garage where we could have put a beat-up old desk. We
got by without a proper office because our job consisted
almost exclusively of going door to door from one
watering hole to the next, receiving orders on our cell
phones, and moving crates of fritz from our relatives'

basements to our clients. As soon as we had filled the first binder with copies of invoices and had to start a second, though, my 12-square-meter dorm room became a little snug.

Since we had to print an address on the bottles of fritz-kola, we used the address of the college dorm for quite a while — even after we had our first warehouse. That once led to a distributor's heavy cargo truck rolling into our narrow residential street, parking right in the middle, and the driver coming into our common room with his freight list asking where he could pick up the fritz-kola. Everyone had a good laugh, and then I went with him to our warehouse in Ellerbek.

The next move was to repurpose Lorenz's two-room apartment in the Eimsbüttel district into an office — a clear violation of the residential zoning code forbidding commercial use, which the statute of limitations has fortunately rendered immaterial. Lorenz moved into a different place, and we simply continued his lease, moving our company in. We remained in this "home/office" until late 2006, even after we had hired an in-office employee and an intern. Were our neighbors to ask, our employees were instructed to tell them that they were Lorenz's cousins, and they were staying with him for a while. Looking back, it was an insane arrangement,

but we couldn't come up with anything better at the time. It was typical of our attitude back then: "Just do it and worry about the details later."

While this was going on, in the summer of 2004, we also rented a warehouse located in a scrapyard in Ellerbek. The family basements were getting too small, and lugging the crates up and down the stairs became no less arduous with time. The warehouse had once been a carpentry workshop, though it was really more of a shed, and it cost 600 euros a month, so it didn't violate our principle of not spending more than we had in the bank. The downside was the lack of heating, requiring us to set up a portable heating unit in the winter so that the bottles wouldn't freeze and explode.

In 2005 we hired a warehouse clerk to receive deliveries, to manage the empties that were returned, and to take care of the initial deliveries to our regular customers. Up to that point, we had been managing all of that on a small scale. We bought a used VW Golf for Norman Sonnrein, our man in the warehouse, and it was our first fleet vehicle. He used it to deliver the kola and receive payment on the spot. Norman was with us for a long time — until we stopped using our own warehouse. At first, he'd wear three layers of clothing in the winter so as not to freeze (to warm up he'd spend time in the restroom, where there was a little space heater), and later he managed the warehouse directly under our offices in Billbrook. Since 2011 our main warehouse has been on the premises of our biggest bottling plant in Wagenfeld, Lower Saxony.

When things finally got too tight in Eimsbüttel, in December 2006 we rented a cheap storefront on Lokstedter Steindamm, a noisy trunk road north of the city center. It consisted of one big room. Our desks were in one corner — we each had our own now that we finally had enough room. Major progress. But we still hadn't instituted any real division of labor. Everyone had to be able to do everything and then to actually do it. It was a constant process of trial and error for all of us.

We had steeled ourselves to the fact that the life of an entrepreneur basically means lots-n-lots of work with little free time. Once the business really started to gain momentum, I had the submission deadline for my bachelor's thesis postponed. As was to be expected, friendships, relationships, and sleep drew the short straws. There simply wasn't time. We'd work until late at night and wake up early in the morning to get back to work. When I finally did get around to sleeping, I was dead to the world. Laying awake at night plagued by worries or getting up to take a nighttime jog came later, after we had built something, had real skin in the game,

and were bearing the responsibility for ever-more employees.

We didn't really know how much work it would turn out to be, nor what kind of tasks we were signing ourselves up for. That was probably for the best, because it allowed us to grow with the job.

We definitely had to learn a lot, and we relied on our very first business plan, the loose-leaf sheet, for a long time. (We didn't come up with a more sophisticated strategy until 2011.) We met each new challenge with a blank expression, at least at first. How do you write invoices, and how can you automate the process? What does the bottling plant need to know? How do you deal with customer complaints? Where is the spare key to the warehouse? How do you get your hands on used bottles and crates, and who'll produce new ones for you? Who prints labels and in what quality? Does VAT apply to the money paid in deposit on empties? (Yes, for sales to distributors; no, for sales to consumers. Madness!) How do you register a fleet vehicle? And so on and so forth.

Some jobs were just a complete turnoff for us. That's why we outsourced the bookkeeping to an accountant soon after the start. Doing so kept the taxman off our backs, and it freed up time for more interesting pursuits, like exploring Amsterdam and delivering kola to clubs.

Interns and pioneers

Katharin Rehder joined us in 2009, initially for an internship that was part of her degree program. Over time, she's become one of my most trusted staff members. Katharin says that she can still smell the odor of that one executive office, the one in the Liebig St. offices located on Hamburg's industrial east side, where we moved in 2008. Thanks to the air conditioning, which was perpetually *kaput*, the place often reeked of a stench something like a mix of kohlrabi and garlic. She also remembers the threadbare carpet, the cheap Ikea furniture, and how the broken sunshades and the huge, south-facing windows amplified the summer heat. But she stuck with us. Following her internship as a student trainee, she joined us in the office, responsible for individual teams in sales, purchasing, and production. She eventually became my right hand when it came to numbers, analysis, and company-wide initiatives. We entrusted her with commercial power of attorney in 2016. She's a shining example of where an internship can lead. When handled properly and fairly, internships should always involve give and take; in my view, they're a win-win deal. The company gains very cheap or even free labor, but from someone who first needs training. In

return, the intern gains a low-risk opportunity to try new things, to learn very, very quickly, and to prove themselves with the prospect of obtaining a permanent position. Sure, some industries got carried away at the turn of the millennium. Members of the "internship generation" would complete one unpaid internship after another, and companies were unfairly cheating them out of the wages that their growing qualifications would certainly have justified.

One thing Katharin liked in her first year was that there were no typical "intern duties." The rule (which usually worked) was: whoever takes the last of the coffee brews the next pot, regardless of whether it was Lorenz, me, or anybody else. We also made our own copies without calling in an intern to do it. At the same time though, Katharin says, the staff would treat each other with less than the utmost courtesy and restraint: "Women at fritz need razor-sharp tongues. It won't do to be overly sensitive." The advantage is that problems and conflicts are raised directly and frankly.

Another memorable aspect of the early years was our extreme frugality. Katharin remembers a dramatic crisis meeting that Lorenz and I had called with some staff because we were having to order staplers *again*. We were of the opinion that enough of these three-euro gadgets must be floating around, although our gum flapping probably wasted 10 to 20 staplers' worth of our staff's time. Katharin herself can relate another typical scene from those years:

There was little time to chat during my internship, but there were two weeks in January when you were able to catch your breath. I remember one time I was sitting on a desk, and a couple of coworkers assigned to Hamburg sales weren't doing much either for a moment, and we were chatting with bottles of fritz in our hands. We couldn't have been at it long, but I could feel Mirco's anxious gaze. Eventually, he came over to us beaming, acted as if he were following the conversation, and then after a few minutes he said to us with a smile and a nod, "What do you say we all get back to work?" I have to admit that I couldn't help laughing. And I can still remember him standing there, and I could tell that he was struggling with himself on the inside. On the one hand, he didn't want to play the boss man, but on the other he really wanted the chit chat to stop. It's a typical dichotomy: having to exert authority when you really want to be a friend.

Katharin remembers something else: anglicisms were utterly avoided at fritz back then. Laptops were called *Klapprechner* ("folding computers"), a flyer was called a *Flugblatt* ("flying sheet"), and so on, which sometimes posed a challenge for new hires. We weren't doing it for

any silly nationalist reasons. The proliferation of bullshit terms, which were gaining popularity in the 2000s and were often severely misunderstood or misinterpreted, simply annoyed us. The slogan used in those years by Douglas, a chain of cosmetics stores, provides a famous example: "Come in and find out." A street poll back then showed that many people thought they were being invited to a maze. And most people aren't too keen on going in somewhere if they're not sure they'll be able to find the way out again. A classic case of shooting oneself in the bullshit-covered foot. We wanted our language to always be simple, clear, and super easy to understand. We didn't want to exclude anyone because their English maybe wasn't good enough or they didn't have a college degree.

Our office equipment in those first years reflected our tight finances. Each of us had our personal laptop and cell phone. One of our first purchases was a fax machine to help us communicate with our bottlers. Beyond that, we bought an old computer and a printer for the warehouse to print invoices for the beverage distributors making pickups. For anyone not producing in-house with their own machines, vehicles are usually the biggest capital outlay. Our constantly growing sales force out on the road needed to be mobile, especially as we expanded into new

areas. The lease vehicles our salespeople would drive were initially pretty small, more compact hatchbacks than mid-size and luxury station wagons, so the biggest outlay in those first few years were the bottles and crates. We started with 300 black crates that — to save money — weren't even printed with the fritz-kola logo. Once we noticed that too many crates were going missing because the lack of a logo made it hard for people to tell where they came from, we started labeling them with stickers. We also bought used crates from other beverage producers and slapped our stickers on them, which we hired a schoolkid to do for us.

The lack of branded fritz-kola crates sometimes drove us to extraordinary lengths. Occasionally, we would transport full bottles of fritz-kola to customers in beer crates we borrowed from breweries, tediously remove the empty fritz bottles out of our own branded crates in the customer's storage room, wipe our crates down with window cleaner, refill them with full bottles from the borrowed beer crates, and take the beer crates loaded with empty bottles with us when we left. This allowed the branded crates with the fritz-kola logo to remain with our customers, preventing other suppliers from taking them by accident.

Sascha Müller joined fritz-kola in 2010 as an outside sales representative, and he was one of our first 20 employees. He was 23 years old, and he had completed his vocational training as a retail salesperson at the Edeka supermarket chain before working there for a few years. He's now an official legend at fritz because he's such a seasoned veteran. That fritz-kola is available in super-markets and beverage stores now is largely thanks to his efforts. We have sat together often and reminisced about how it all began. With a satisfied grin, he likes to recall how he became responsible for the entire sales region of northern Germany overnight, without any experience selling out in the field. We took a shotgun approach to selecting customers because it was the only way we could even attempt to cover all the regions. Sascha would be in Hamburg one day, in Wolfsburg the next, in Bremen the day after, and so on. At first, he drove all those routes in his own personal VW Polo, with the company paying him a mileage allowance because we couldn't afford another vehicle lease. Once he inherited a coworker's company car in 2011, he felt like he had finally arrived at fritz, as he likes to tell to this day.

Patrick Keller was another forerunner. He worked in our sales and marketing department from 2008 until 2012, before heading down to Switzerland for personal reasons. When we hired him, our company counted three interns, one account manager, two sales representatives on the road throughout Hamburg, a handful of freelance sales representatives, Norman in the warehouse, and Lorenz and me. Patrick had trained as a banker, but he'd since started pursuing a degree in sociology. He did merchandising on the side, running the merch tables and selling t-shirts at concerts. He met Lorenz in 2006 at one of those events and asked for an internship. We had set up a fritz-kola refrigerator in the backstage area of a concert being held in the Hamburg Stadtpark. It was one of our first sponsorship gigs. The idea was that the road crews from Germany and around the world would get to know the real Hamburg kola and raise our profile well beyond the city.

Patrick fit right in, especially with Lorenz. The two of them shared a passion for Nike sneakers that they parlayed into partnerships with sneaker-related events and Oliver Korittke's sneaker museum in Berlin along with ads in *Sneaker Freaker* magazine.

Patrick's "job interview" took place in our tiny, crammed office on Lokstedter Steindamm, and it lasted five minutes. He remembers how I was leaning against my desk and asked "So do you wanna work here or what?" He had the feeling that I was in a good mood but still somewhat skeptical. But of course, Lorenz and I had already discussed it, and there was no doubt that we would take him on as an intern. On that day, we prepared the ground for a new era at fritz-kola. Besides Patrick, we also hired a sales representative for the St. Pauli district of Hamburg and two more interns. We were ready for the future.

Let's let Patrick wrap his story up himself:

Having worked at fritz definitely looks good on a resumé. And I learned so much. Especially about taking responsibility and initiative. At a very young age, I was able to contribute to a company breaking into the market, make decisions, and take responsibility for them, which I wouldn't have been able to do elsewhere. Mirco and Lorenz lived according to the Boy-Scout principle of "youth leading youth." They hired lots of young people who shared a mindset similar to their own, and they trusted them.

fritzes also had a preternatural talent for partying. My birthday usually coincided with the Internorga, one of the most important food and beverage trade shows worldwide, and it takes place in Hamburg. We would often party all night long on my birthday, and then we'd have to man the booth the next morning. Once I was still so blasted that Lorenz banished me behind the curtain to do some client data entry. Dealing with the public wouldn't have been a good idea on that day. Mirco wasn't a fan of getting carried away like that at trade shows. He wanted all the expense that went into the booth to pay off and for as many attendees of the trade show as possible to have tried fritz-kola by the end.

Mirco and I took a few trips to foreign cities, like London and Amsterdam. Mirco would say things like "Keller, all the trends start in London. We should go back and take a closer look." It was cool, but these weren't just booze cruises. Mirco is simply never off duty. We'd often storm through the town, hitting 20 potential clients by midnight without even stopping for a bite to eat. But I was used to that from Hamburg, where, if Mirco and I entered a place and he got that panicked look in his eyes, he'd say "Oh, we're not even on the menu here."

It's dangerous to go alone

The decision not to seek out food chemists and to produce fritz-kola ourselves was certainly a wise one. For one thing, we couldn't have afforded building a plant, keeping everything clean, the logistics, and so on. Outsourcing production allowed us to delegate the entire area of food regulation and supervision to bottling operations that had more experience with it. We are fortunate to live in a country where we can trust that — aside from the odd scandal — the food we buy won't kill us or make us sick. There are agencies monitoring things like hygiene, ingredients, and whatnot. But it comes at considerable expense. A company like Bionade could afford such things because it grew out of a brewery that already had the necessary plant and procedures. But we were green as could be, without capital or expertise. Our ignorance was revealed spectacularly in the summer of 2003.

We had just brought a fresh shipment back to Hamburg and stowed it away when we noticed something odd. Weird flakes were floating around in the kola and, looking at the necks of the bottles, it was apparent that the liquid at the top had lost its color. What was that about? Kola with extra pulp? And what were we supposed to do about it? Although we had customers waiting for resupply, we also knew that, if we showed up with a brand-new kola that looked even slightly dubious, we'd be finished. If we were going to build and establish a successful new kola brand, the quality had to be consistently good. It's bad enough for an established brand to lose trust through a lapse in quality control, but for the new brand on the block it's the kiss of death. This shipment was definitely not going to win us new customers, and it probably would have cost us our existing ones. Gaining credibility in the hospitality business was tough enough already.

We called the brewery. The master brewer assured us that what we observed would produce no ill health effects and that the kola was perfectly safe to drink. But that was out of the question. We couldn't have been more frustrated. As usual back then, we had sunk almost all of our money into the botched batch, but we resolved not to dump it on our customers in that state. We lacked any experience in dealing with suppliers and with such difficult, practically life-and-death situations. How could we express our complaint without aggravating the master brewer so badly that we'd lose our supplier?

It's important to note that purchasing only small batches doesn't entitle you to much. The big, industrial-sized bottlers didn't care about us. They aren't going to

reset their machines for a new product or even turn them on for a few hundred crates. So we had no choice but to deal with the smaller, more artisanal operations, and they can't always deliver the same consistently high quality.

Fortunately, the master brewer convinced the regional sales manager of his own supplier to serve as the mediator in our talks to find a solution, and thus he laid the cornerstone of a friendship that continues to connect fritz and that regional sales manager, Peter Thiele. Here's how Peter tells it:

Because I've been with them since the beginning, I've had the uncommon luck to serve as supplier, advisor, cofounder, employee, multiplier, developer, networker, supporter, motivator, sympathizer, mediator, broker, communicator, introducer, confidant, counselor, companion, and on and on and on — and a good friend to both founders.

Peter even took a detour on the way to his summer vacation for this meeting in the brewery. While his wife tried to wrangle and entertain their two kids for hours, Lorenz and I sat with Peter and the master brewer in the wood-paneled parlor of the small estate brewery, which only brewed soft drinks on the side and had been using ingredients from Peter's company practically forever.

We had come resolved to have our demands met, including replacement for the faulty batch at no charge.

Our ignorance of the production process unsettled us, so we asked detailed questions about it. We really wanted to understand what had gone wrong. Moreover, we simply couldn't afford to write off the bad batch of kola and pay for a whole new one. Peter performed a diplomatic balancing act. He naturally wanted to avoid embarrassment on the part of his customer, whose own tight financial situation he understood well. On the other hand, though, he seemed to take to Lorenz and me right away, and most of all he took us seriously. He recognized that we were negotiating for the life of our "baby," which had absorbed all of our money, sweat, and tears. He also understood that the business we had just started stood on the precipice, so a solution was desperately required. Peter wanted to help even smaller clients that were just starting out to receive the best service and top quality. After all, everyone starts off small, and rookies rely on veterans' professionalism. He also recognized fritz-kola's potential, and he knew that we might grow to be a very big customer someday. He was wise to trust his instincts.

After the four-way talks proved fruitless — the master brewer wasn't budging — Peter tried talking to each side individually. Eventually, he managed to achieve an agreement: we would bring the botched batch back to the

brewery at our own cost, and then a new batch would be quickly produced under Peter's supervision. And Peter's company was going to donate the ingredients. It was a solution that allowed both sides to minimize their losses and to save face. We were very grateful. The ingredients are a major cost factor, particularly for small batches. Another clause in the "Face-Saving Treaty" was that the question of what had actually gone wrong would no longer be discussed.

I advise all founders to err on the side of being perfectionistic and hypercritical at first when it comes to quality control. At least that's the case for any food products and those with health-relevant effects, which have to be flawless if they are to avoid endangering anyone. In other areas, one can probably get by with a little more trial and error, adhering more to the motto of "better done than perfect." Nevertheless, if your new product fails to impress, you can blow even the most carefully prepared market launch.

Meeting Peter was sheer luck. He was competent and fair, and he quickly became our friend and fan. He was one of the first to champion fritz-kola in his own circle, at New Year's Eve parties and other social events. He was also one of the first to notice how strong and attractive our brand really was. And Peter always clued us in to developments he observed on the market, like the phenomenon of "melon soda."

After the affair with the inconsistent quality, we started looking around for a new bottling plant, one with more experience with soft drinks and a more careful approach. But it would also have to be small enough to handle small quantities regularly and competently. It wasn't easy to find a supplier to fit that bill, but we finally did manage to find a bottling plant between Hannover and Dortmund that agreed to work with us. This bottler would allow us to get started producing up to a truckload — nearly 32,000 bottles — per week.

Our needs grew faster than that bottling plant could manage, so in 2006, we switched to another bottler located in the Ruhr valley. In those first few years, bottling fritz-kola demanded a lot of attention. Smaller, lovingly run artisanal operations were happy to welcome a little kola startup with low production volumes. They could manage the smaller batches, but they also expected their clients to accept a greater margin of error, perhaps in the form of too much or too little carbonation or bottles filled to visibly different levels. As we grew, so did our customers' standards, and we ended up changing bottling plants rather frequently. Looking back, I fondly remember the fritz-kola of those days and how it was practically handmade.

The experience with our first bottler might have made us hypersensitive regarding quality control. Joachim Fink learned that firsthand when he became our bottler for southern Germany and Austria for four years soon after our start. At the time, our bottles in southern Germany bore labels reading "Hamburg salutes the South." Joachim had a little bottling plant in Lingenau, near Bregenz in Austria and very close to Lake Constance, and he had only six employees. Among other clients, they bottled the famous *Almdudler*, a carbonated Austrian herbal beverage, for a while.

We came together in a rather curious fashion — at the other end of the world in Alaska. A friend of Joachim's mother had emigrated there 40 years previously. Since her last name was Fritz, she googled this (relatively common) name frequently. By 2004 we had apparently climbed far enough in the search results for her to stumble across us, and she told Joachim about this kola company in Hamburg. Since he was hunting for clients at the time anyway, he sent us an email asking politely and directly whether we were looking for a bottling plant.

Here's how Joachim remembers our first meeting:
They answered quickly, and shortly thereafter Mirco and

Lorenz stopped by in their Golf to look at our operation and negotiate. I found them pleasantly modest — my clients usually drive up in fancy cars and flash their expensive watches and phones. The two of them were pretty reserved at first, and compared to us they seemed a little icy, as northerners tend to be. They obviously lacked experience in that kind of negotiation, but they believed in their product and negotiated with confidence. Since dealing with Coca-Cola didn't appeal to me and I found the conglomerate to be fairly disagreeable, I was happy to see someone new on the market, and I made them a fair price.

The small quantities that we initially required — only 60 to 80 crates — were a challenge for Joachim. They were partially shipped to us in Hamburg by truck, and Joachim would personally drive some to Stuttgart and unload them at a warehouse in dicey circumstances. That was the supply hub for the still very small market in southern Germany. But soon there was a central storage facility in Stuttgart.

Joachim himself can best describe how personal and informal our cooperation was in those early years:

My usual contact at fritz tended to be Lorenz. We had a very good relationship, more like buddies than business associates. Lorenz visited us regularly down in the mountains of Vorarlberg. I was always ready to discuss open questions with

him, and he also enjoyed the atmosphere in the Vorarlberg region. That's why we'd usually go out to eat Käsknöpfle, which is the local term for a dish rather like a good macaroni and cheese, ride down the summer bobsled track, and then take the gondola up the mountain to drink a beer or two.

By the way, Lorenz always ordered a crate of fritz-kola that we had brewed for him because he found that the alpine water made it taste better.

I also went to Hamburg a few times. I remember May of 2008, when Lorenz and I partied for three days in gorgeous weather on the beaches of the Baltic Sea. We just hit one dance club after another.

When it came to work, some things on the fritz-kola side were pretty chaotic. When Norman, the warehouse manager in Hamburg, would place an order with me, it was often the case that we didn't have enough crates or bottles or that they had forgotten to send us the ingredients. They seemed to love changing the quantities and deadlines for their orders, and they did so often. It could get hectic and pretty annoying at times.

A lack of crates and bottles didn't always result from poor organization. At first, they simply didn't have the money to buy the stuff. Once I even loaned them 3,000 euros for crates and bottles, which they paid off bit by bit. Looking back, I would have preferred a few shares in the company …

We unfortunately stopped working together in September 2008. The sugar from our new sugar supplier would crystallize and make flakes in the kola. It was only a cosmetic issue — it didn't have any health effects, nor did it alter the flavor. But fritz nevertheless terminated our relationship very suddenly.

There had been a few small issues prior to that because we couldn't always fill the bottles to exactly the same level. After all, we're just a little artisanal operation, and we don't have a computer-controlled industrial plant. But we always did our work properly, and we've never had any problems with mold or germs.

I have since rekindled my good relationships with fritz and Mirco. We distribute throughout Austria, and we sell fritz-kola. The brand was hard to find here for a long time, but with our new sales representative, you can usually find it at least in the college towns. But there remains a strong disparity between north and south — the kola from Hamburg is still more popular among those fish-heads up north.

From 2006 until 2010, we used a small brewery in western Germany to serve northern and central Germany. It was somewhat larger than the previous brewery, the staff were highly motivated, and the hissing, steaming plant was practically an antique. But it did produce top-quality fritz-kola. The brewery came to us around the spring of 2010, and they divulged that they were shutting down their plant, but they also wanted to set up a new bottling plant in the next town on the premises of a disused beverage factory. In order to do so, they were looking to found a new company with someone else in the beverage industry. It sounded good at first — newer, better, more storage space. So we told them to get enough product ready in advance and then to get on with the move. But nobody could have expected the following summer of extreme opposites. First came the scorching heat wave during soccer's monthlong World Cup of soccer; then came the wettest August since meteorological record-keeping began in 1881. Such drastic swings are a real challenge for the beverage industry because they make it difficult to manage the inventory of available product.

Massive problems arose following the move from the brewery into the new factory. We had grown considerably. In 2008 we took out our first bank loan to finance the launch of our new 200 ml bottle. We had new offices, we had rented a big, new warehouse in Hamburg, and we had hired a bunch of new fritzes. We were saddled with sizeable monthly fixed costs. We couldn't afford to be constantly visiting our bottlers and looking over their shoulders to avoid problems. But the problems and "bottlenecks" just kept coming. Distributors were stuck waiting on our product with increasing frequency, and we'd have to stall them for a few days. One time at the plant, the new storage tanks from Asia were *kaput*, then something got damaged, then the new control module for the plant went "on the fritz." It was just one problem after another. It turned out that the plant was being cobbled together from new and used parts. There's nothing wrong with that approach in principle, but it can make for a less reliable system. The brewery's old plant might have been antediluvian, but at least it got the job done. Every possible flaw had either been fixed over the generations or they had grown familiar to their problems and the solutions to them. Now, with the new plant, we found ourselves sitting on a pile of empty bottles ever-more often. The unfilled orders were gradually turning into a crisis.

Could these problems have been related to the new co-owners from the beverage industry? Due to the constant problems in the bottling plant, they took on another partner, who also indirectly held some stock in our competition. I can't say any more about the true causes of our enormous problems. We were indeed fighting for survival, and maybe I was just imagining things. At the time, we were receiving reports that other

non-alcoholic beverages were being produced at the same bottling plant in sufficient quantities and that their sales were rising. What could we do? We were already burning the candle at both ends, and a lawsuit wasn't going to help, so we desperately needed a new bottling plant.

Fortunately, and unrelated to this fiasco, we had found another new partner in northern Germany. Coincidentally, the plant had been built after the reunification of Germany to produce a different cola but had lost that client overnight. Then we showed up on their doorstep. Everyone in the operation knew their way around cola and soft drinks, and not only were they highly motivated, but they also had a well-oiled, functioning bottling plant. We weren't able to fill all the orders in 2010, and especially in the summer we spent many weeks with an empty warehouse and disappointed customers. We didn't sell a bottle of some varieties for weeks. But thanks to the plant in Mecklenburg, we usually had our fritz-kola in stock.

The situation with the bottler in western Germany kept getting worse, and the losses just kept growing. If we hadn't found the operation in the northeast, the lost revenue might have cost us our entire business. So we licked our wounds and allowed our bottling contract with the unreliable partner to expire at the end of 2010. We said our thank-yous and got our wagon train moving again.

What did I learn from that crisis? First, entrepreneurs should never naïvely fool themselves into believing that new automatically means better. Regardless of whether it's about software or a production plant, the enthusiasm of engineers and developers is one thing, but reality is another. Of course, innovation is vital, and there's no way to avoid teething troubles, but when it comes to a new setup, you should plan on double the time and expense that you're quoted. If things happen to go more smoothly than expected, then great.

Another lesson is to always examine new business partners, to consider what interests they might have, and whether they might be in bed with the competition. It saves nasty surprises. The same applies to changes in the ownership structure. Who am I dealing with and what interests are they pursuing? Since we still don't have our own bottling plant, even many years later, we certainly haven't seen the last of this issue. I now know that some characters will deliberately target their competition's network. That could be a bottling plant or any other kind of supplier or service provider. They'll offer lucrative deals to those willing to betray their associates. After six months, though, they'll stop ordering as much or anything at all. By that time, however, the damage will have been done, and the companies they've used won't be able

to simply go back to their old clients, whose trust they've violated and who have probably already found replacements. By the time the truth comes out and the sabotage has been revealed, it's usually too late. Sometimes business is a full-contact sport.

Since early 2011 we've been working with the Auburg-Quelle spring water company, which is based in Lower Saxony and belongs to the family of Dirk Lütvogt. It wasn't easy to gain Dirk as a partner. On our epic quest for a perfect bottling network for fritz-kola, I spoke to a representative of his company at a trade show. I asked whether they could put me in touch with whoever was in charge of subcontracting their bottling. I was told I could forget about it. They already had a partnership with another cola company. A little while later I was visiting a keg-filling plant because we were looking to serve ready-made fritz-kola in kegs at big festivals. This was even trickier than finding someone to bottle soft drinks in glass bottles, but Dirk had the right kind of plant. So I tried my luck and contacted him directly. As it turned out, he was in the process of planning a brand-new plant for reusable glass bottles, and he was looking for clients that could serve as the cornerstone of his new multi-million-euro investment. Bingo! We had several years of steady growth and healthy revenue, which are important criteria to anyone looking for a partner to help shoulder that kind of outlay. Someone out there was prepared to build us a brand-new bottling plant for our reusable glass bottles. fritz-kola would always be available and in exquisite quality. Finally! It felt great to have someone in the beverage industry who finally believed in us and was prepared to shell out a very large sum of money in advance. That moment really was a turning point in the evolution of fritz-kola.

On January 19, 2011, the first bottles filled with fritz-kola came out of the machines, and those were the very first bottles filled by this first-class, sustainable, new plant. To me, it felt like a reward for all of our team's hard work, for the women and men serving our hospitality and retail customers 24/7. We had worked so hard for so many years to get our kola out into the world, often having to use old plants to produce it, and now finally it was being bottled by the best of the best. In that same year, the plant won the Innovation in Reusability Award from the Environmental Action Germany organization and the Reusability Initiative Foundation (*Stiftung Initiative Mehrweg*). Having helped us to grow with his Auburg spring since 2011, it was only natural for Dirk Lütvogt to join us as a new equity holder of fritz-kola in 2017, which has solidified his place in our company's story.

güstrow

wagenfeld

gänsefurth

sersheim

siegsdorf

Since 2010, a year marked by our existential crisis and concerns about having enough sellable product on hand, we've managed to significantly improve our decentralized network of local bottlers that accept reusable bottles. In 2021 as this book is being published, five independently operated bottling plants throughout central Europe are working to manufacture fritz-kola products using green energy, reusable packaging, and modern equipment. We, as the independent kola brand, are now also at the center of a network of independent bottling operations.

I am so grateful for all the elbow grease that so many fritzes and our partners have invested to get our kola into the bottle, just because they believed in a couple of college kids.

what other people know

When speaking on the topic of founding a business, the most common question I'm asked is how to get good advice and from whom. And it's one of the few questions where I don't just cheerfully recommend following the example of how we got started in business. Looking back, I would say that we were certainly a little naïve. We just wanted to get our project underway and learn how to go about being entrepreneurs. And we had no time whatsoever for neurotics, negative hangers-on, or skeptics. That's why we avoided asking anyone for help or advice for the first few years.

After several years of running my own business, I've since changed my mind. Usually, it's simply smarter to ask others for their opinions and advice. If someone

expresses doubts or even tries to talk you out of the project explicitly, you simply have to live with it. At the end of the day, only your own conscience and judgment can guide you. Decisions made in consultation with others are simply more substantial and have undergone greater scrutiny.

We were taking on a global conglomerate, and we didn't think to obtain any advice about the financial or legal implications (especially relating to trademarks). And as mentioned above, we initially chose a mode of incorporation that would have left us personally liable in the event of poor economic performance. We didn't even know at the time that we would have only had to deposit half of the 25,000 euros in equity capital required to register an LLC, so it wasn't nearly as unobtainable as we thought. We just thought "Screw it" and got moving. Our motto was "We're clueless, but we're going to do it anyway." There was also a bit of "We're way too small to show up on their radar anyway." And our basic outlook was something like "It'll all work out."

That's often a good attitude to have. At least it's better than constant hesitation and wanting to rule out all possible misfortunes before actually doing anything. You can also plan things to death. And we weren't responsible for any employees or families back then, which would have made our brash approach seriously negligent. In general, it's definitely a good idea to become familiar with the relevant rules and regulations before starting a complex undertaking. Moreover, I would advise any founder to take advantage of the advice and support programs offered by banks and chambers of commerce, often at no charge. In Berlin there's even a municipal founder hotline sponsored by the Senate Department for Economics. You can also simply ask other founders. There are plenty of them out there, and they're easy to find on the internet. Many are surprisingly willing to meet and chat over a cold kola and to provide some useful pointers.

Most of the mistakes we made because we failed to seek advice didn't occur during the founding stage, but later. And they related to the classic management topics. If we had sought out experienced practitioners as mentors, we might have been able to perform better in our leadership roles and organized the company and our procedures better. We waited far too long to seek external advice and expertise. We grossly overestimated ourselves. Had we secured outside help in the form of mentors or advisors, I'm sure that we could have managed the subsequent crises better or perhaps even avoided them completely.

I've been taking advantage of opportunities to converse with other entrepreneurs, creative people, and coaches since the shareholder structure of our company changed in 2016/17. It's easy to grab the chance on the fringes of business gatherings and seminars. I often find that others have already faced the same issue or question, and they've already tried out some potential solutions. As is so often the case, talking helps.

Another thing we completely ignored back then were the laws and regulations that could affect our business. Aside from the commercial license and trademark registration, we went in completely uninformed, taking a stance of "If they want something from us, they're sure to find us." Since our business consisted mostly of buying and reselling product, that approach was just barely acceptable because we outsourced the most heavily regulated processes to our producers, shippers, and bottlers.

It almost seemed like the punishment for our ignorance was nipping at our heels. In 2008 we set up some tables and chairs in our new, nearly empty warehouse to welcome our many new fritzes and introduce them to the company. Suddenly, we heard someone in the freight elevator fumbling with the key in the door outside our room, and a strange guy popped in. He was a consumer safety inspector, and he was already gloating like a train conductor who had just found a passenger without a ticket. He had received an anonymous tip that we were producing beverages illegally, so he very surreptitiously got a key from the building superintendent. He wanted to catch us red handed. His delight quickly deteriorated into disappointment and then a hasty retreat once we explained to him that we simply sold the beverages without mixing them ourselves. Once he was thoroughly convinced that there really wasn't a secret *Breaking Bad* lab hidden somewhere in the room, he hit the road.

That man with his delusions of grandeur were the only negative (well, funny really) encounter with the authorities. Otherwise, we've found the agencies in Hamburg that are responsible for the economy, like the tax bureau and the local councils, to be consistently helpful and encouraging. Based on what we've heard from other countries, we can count ourselves in Germany fortunate to have such predictable and constructive government agencies.

By the way, that silly encounter with Safety Inspector Gadget does touch on a fairly serious subject. Our story — two college students take on Coca-Cola — gave many people the impression that we were mixing the kola ourselves. At first, we found the running gag about the first bottles being filled out of a jury-rigged bathtub-cum-mixing vat so amusing that we didn't put much effort into correcting anyone who disbelievingly asked about the story. We assumed that the gag was too silly for anyone to take it seriously.

But we soon noticed that some people couldn't get that image out of their head, and it wasn't doing our business any favors. Those buying and serving our beverage naturally wanted to be sure that this new invention was being professionally produced in impeccably hygienic conditions. Considering the typical state of college students' bathrooms and the thought that the same tub would be used for bathing and making kola, the urban legend was no longer funny or a marketing gimmick; it was just gross. That's why it was so important for our sales representatives to make a good impression. We would always tell them to keep their cars clean and to wear decent clothes. Show up to the customer well-groomed because they have to believe that they're ordering a proper kola from you, not some poison. A kola they'll be proud to serve their guests.

While we're talking appearances, I, too, had to give some thought occasionally to what was expected of an entrepreneur. Could I show up to an appointment at the bank in jeans and a t-shirt? Since we had sworn not to go into debt, that question didn't come up until 2007. I opted to wear a sports coat to an important meeting with my account manager at the *Hamburger Sparkasse* bank one time, and I felt like I was wearing a costume. I was very relieved afterwards when he said to me, "Would you please wear a t-shirt again next time? Don't worry about it."

People also often ask me about my role models, about the entrepreneurial personalities that have inspired me. Richard Branson, the founder of Virgin Music, was an important figure for a long time. For the younger readers, Branson was the Elon Musk of the closing twentieth century. He started out — simply and without much capital outlay — importing vinyl records and then opening record stores. It gradually grew into a very well-diversified business with an airline and whatnot. The business is a pony that knows many tricks, not just one. I liked the Virgin story, and Branson impressed me for a long time, not the least because he also stood up for economic and social change as well as environmental conservation (although the environmental side does clash a bit with running an airline). The other, much more tangible role model was my father because he exemplified to me a passion for independence and entrepreneurship. It's a passion that can move mountains and, most of all, recognizes opportunities instead of problems and obstacles.

welcome to the wake up

Now, I usually run into fritz when I least expect it, like a few summers ago in a little kiosk in a lonely mountain village on the island of Mallorca. The top priority has always been world domination.

jana hollenberg, former marketing manager

When they think of marketing, many people think of colorful pictures and billboards. Sure, they're part of marketing, but I would start with the four Ps of the marketing mix: product, price, place, and promotion. What product am I selling for what price in which place with what kind of promotional communication?

In our very first, one-page plan for fritz-kola, we laid the groundwork for our marketing strategy. We were going to sell kola that was less sweet, with more caffeine, in single-serving glass bottles (the product), to cafés, bars, restaurants, and clubs … everywhere people — especially college students — go to have a good time (place). When it came to price, it was immediately clear that we had to take our cue from the competition. Before the invention of social media) our very scant financial means left us with only one-on-one communication, which meant talking to people. If people talk about us when we're not around, that's even better.

Helpfully, our original plan contained something whose significance we had barely begun to realize: purpose (a fifth P!) — what's the use of fritz-kola? As friends and college students, we wanted "to do our thing," be independent, and coincidentally keep ourselves awake with caffeine. As our success grew and we gained greater recognition, it started to dawn on us that we could really make some meaningful change, like pushing reusable glass bottles instead of single-use, recyclable, plastic ones, and taking a stance on social issues. Later, we learned that we could even convince farmers to transition from growing conventional rhubarb to organic if we agreed to long-term purchase guarantees. We only really became conscious of our purpose through our fans. We saw what people were associating us with in their feedback, in surveys, and in conversations. People started applying to us for jobs because they wanted to share in our purpose, our mission, and our stance.

So when do we get to the campaigns with all the pictures and commotion? We didn't have the money or the patience for all that in the first few years. All we really did was to tell countless people about our kola and give them sample bottles.

At some point, a rumor started to spread that Lorenz and I were using guerilla marketing tactics. We allegedly left a couple crates of fritz-kola in a university elevator or in the dorm, hoping that some takers would be happy enough with the freebies to remember the brand, keep their eyes peeled, and eventually start asking about it. We never did that, but it is a nice story. One thing we did do was to ask our friends to order fritz-kola when they went

out and drum up some demand. It was really quite effective in our limited stomping grounds around Hamburg.

marketing & activism

One of the first opportunities to raise our kola's profile and to do some good came in 2007 with the G8 summit in Heiligendamm. We had the honor of supplying two activist camps with free fritz-kola. It wasn't much yet, but it was what we could manage at the time. Our commitment to preventing climate change and protecting human rights is something we shared in the earliest phase, when we were still the "garage kola" and had no capacity to influence anything.

Years later at the 2017 G20 summit in Hamburg, we were able to engage with social issues more intensively and to support Hamburg's critical voices. Our material support consisted of complimentary beverage deliveries to various protest events, like the "1000 Figures" (*1000 Gestalten*) march, which featured a crowd of people covered in gray proceeding through the city center. We were also on the scene with free kola at the "Collective Cooking in the Millerntor Gallery" event, at the demonstration on the Heiliggeistfeld fairgrounds, at the

"Get up – Stand Up" event that took place at the Spiel-budenplatz as well as in the media center, at the protest camps, and at the wrap-up event. And we joined the ranks of those sponsoring the "Democracy Festival."

Our billboards that read "hey man, wake up!" (*mensch, wach auf!*) are surely what garnered us the most attention. The Blood ad agency came up with the motif, which the Hamburg artist Sutosuto turned into a reality and was visible on billboards throughout Germany. We commissioned drawings of the world's most powerful politicians asleep, but we deliberately avoided denigrating, caricaturing, or mocking them. The message was that sleeping, doing nothing, is not an option when facing such a broad range of global problems. Sleep also fit nicely with a kola containing lots-n-lots of caffeine that will wake you up.

We certainly succeeded in our goal of provoking discussion with our billboards. People still approach us to this day asking about our involvement in those events. Attention is a currency that we at fritz-kola know how to spend. However, the rose of attention has its thorns too, which is something we have to accept. The depiction of President Erdogan of Turkey asleep unleashed a colossal shitstorm of social-media posts, emails, and phone calls. Many refreshment stands and supermarket operators delisted our kola and soft drinks for weeks because they felt our depiction was inappropriate, and they weren't prepared to accept it. We had to deal with the lost revenue and respond sensibly to their hostility. Due to our own apprehension, we closed the offices earlier for a while and worked from home whenever possible until it blew over.

Another issue at the time was the symbiosis of social action and business, which some people appreciated, and others criticized. We understand that we rubbed some people the wrong way with a billboard that read "the only thing better at waking you up is a water cannon" (*nur wasserwerfer machen wacher*), which was backlit and placed at the corner of Susannen St. and Schulterblatt St., right across from the Rote Flora, a squatter house and cultural icon in the leftist movement. A sense of humor probably helps to appreciate the combination of political and commercial interests as something intriguing. I myself am not blind to the ambivalence. We're not seriously trying to claim that consuming soft drinks can be a subversive political act. And these motifs also play a bit with the idea of bouncing back and forth between earnestness and provocation. But consuming fritz-kola is often part of someone taking a stand. The choice to drink it — or not to be caught dead drinking it — often has to do with one's politics. It's deeply related to the mindset of a cosmopolitan, conscious consumer.

The backlit billboard with the water-cannon tagline was removed years ago, by the way. That was also a political decision, but perhaps not in the way you might think. The billboard hung above a green grocer shop, and his lease was canceled. The owner of the property has left it to remain empty for years since. The same is true of a brand-new house across the street, which is a replica of the style popular at the turn of the twentieth century. Nobody knows why these properties remain unused, but they are emblematic of how real estate is irresponsibly wasted in a city with a shortage of living and commercial space.

Our initial cluelessness about advertising is the inverse of our current success with it. We first started thinking about the issue when one of our very first

customers reordered and took the occasion to ask me for a pop-up display. I just stared at him like a deer in the headlights — I had no idea what he was talking about. "A display," he repeated, trying to help me overcome my awkward ignorance. I eventually grasped what he was getting at: something he could set up that would display fritz-kola bottles with our name and logo. Until that point, we had assumed that it was perfectly sufficient for the barkeepers to just plop some bottles on the bar or something. We hadn't given any thought to how the bars could best display fritz-kola. But we quickly caught on that guests should be able to see that this spot sold fritz-kola, and they'd be able to order one without having to consult the menu first. It dawned on us that we should start thinking about promotional materials, like pop-up displays, stickers, and flyers. A tip for rookies who want to sell their product somewhere without standing next to it all day: make sure that promotional and display materials to inform customers that they can buy the product at their current location are available immediately. The materials should reinforce the brand and whet the customers' appetites for the product.

Our customer's request panicked us into action, so we bought some bright yellow cardboard from a stationery store and cobbled together a display. It looked like a piece of junk, and it could only hold two bottles, but it served its purpose and boosted sales. We also designed some fritz stickers and had them printed. We immediately started delivering them along with the crates, and they were also available for sale online to anyone. And we did in fact have fans who would actually order them … for money. They *really* liked us. I'd also go to Ikea from time to time and buy things like mirrors, glass shelves, and other articles that Lorenz and I would repurpose into promotional materials by hand with stickers and paint.

These early, economical forays into point-of-sale (aka point-of-truth) advertising were how we started to supply our hospitality clients with promotional materials. We scaled this activity up so fast that some started to complain of fritz-kola-branding overkill in restaurants and bars. Just six months after getting started, we had enough capital to supply bar owners with fritz-kola refrigerators. We'd buy cheap, new and used refrigerators, color them black with paint or decals, slap a logo on them, and get them out to our customers. Norman, our warehouse guy, would often help us to build and decorate fridges and chalkboards. Gerrit Lerch has said that "For a time, it was impossible to escape those two boys' faces anywhere."

attracting attention

We very gradually began turning our attention to the question of ads and billboards. *Feuer auf St. Pauli* (Fire on St. Pauli), the ad agency that later became RedRabbit, gave us our first ad motif in 2003 or 2004 on spec. It was a "case," which is how agencies show off what creative things they can do besides normal advertising. The motif shows puckered, red lips drinking fritz-kola through a straw, being held in frame by a hand. A second hand is holding a red-and-white fritz-kola in in the frame (it really was a fritz-kola, but in the colors of another, very familiar brand of cola), and it was pouring this one out. Between the two hands, there was a slogan, "drink a fritz instead!" We had posters printed bearing this motif and gave them to our hospitality customers to decorate their walls. Even though we didn't print many, the poster found its way to Coca-Cola. Even though it didn't depict their bottle, the colors made it obvious who we had in mind. We received a letter from Coca-Cola Berlin, their German headquarters. It has unfortunately gone missing, but it came from their general counsel and was written in a friendly tone. We were welcomed into the Germany beverage market, our ad had been seen and noted, but we were asked to please commit in writing that we would never use that motif again. We did so. Just the same, we were pretty proud that the biggest cola in the world had written a letter to kola munchkins like us. We then cut off the offending part of the remaining posters or censored it with a sticker (see image) and passed them around. Waste not, want not.

What inspired an agency to do any work for us on spec? The whole fritz package was apparently an attractive prospect for the ad people: two students bravely enter a market dominated by Coca-Cola, the goliath; our target market consisting of college students and trendy nightspots; and a successful product launch with a logo that tells our startup story. Added to that, interest in the phenomenon of startups was generally growing along with reappreciation for the value of local and regional products instead of global brands.

Among other ideas, the agency also came up with the legendary poster that showed a naked couple having sex, except that there was a horse's head in place of the man's. The tagline read "for long nights. fritz-kola. lots-n-lots of caffeine."

Even though editorial bureaus throughout Germany were offering us free ad space for that motif because they found it so awesome, not everyone was a fan. Today, it would probably land us in a shitstorm of shitstorms. It might be susceptible to accusations of sexism because the couple depicted was straight. Animal rights activists were complaining about it back then — it was something to do with the horse. I think today's greater sensitivity for stereotypes and discriminatory thinking as well as for the rights and needs of disadvantaged and minority groups is a good thing. Advertising should and must adapt to the altered sensibilities that now exist. That's not always easy, especially for brands like fritz that like to use humor, because excluding some group or other is one way humor can work. It's a challenge, but it's one we're happy to meet. Many motifs that we might have found amusing at the turn of the millennium would no longer make it out of the cutting room, and rightly so. Other campaigns poking fun at certain groups, like hippy kids who attended Waldorf schools (see image) and tree huggers, seem to remain acceptable.

Motifs that we wouldn't use anymore do, however, remain part of fritz's history, and part of this book too. As someone who cares about history, I would find a story that omitted anything today's political correctness would deem offensive or unacceptable to be pretty stupid and warped. My overall impression is that it's considerably easier now to attract attention and provoke a reaction with sharp advertising.

In our company's first years, marketing was subordinated to the sales department, without a department of its own. Still, we continued to expand our marketing activities with radio and cinema ads. We worked with the RedRabbit agency for many years to distinguish our brand and build our brand recognition in our target market. The Rocket & Wink and Blood agencies later came to play important roles as well.

After Patrick Keller finished his three-month orientation period as a fritz intern in 2008, he still had to go out and prove himself by gathering experience as a salesperson on the road. We gave him a vehicle and responsibility for a few customers that Lorenz and I had been handling until then in the area in and around Bremen. Our deal with Patrick was simple: you go do sales out on the road for a while, and then you can do the marketing. We were of the opinion that knowing what was going on out there with the customers was a precondition for being good at advertising. There's some truth to that even today, especially because the majority of our advertising was directed at the hospitality industry, whereas today we also target grocery stores, impulse-buy outlets (kiosks, convenience stores, and gas stations), and consumers themselves.

After serving his time in sales, Patrick worked with

other interns on marketing and promotional campaigns, like sponsoring film, music, and surf festivals. He likes to say, with a twinkle in his eye, that our marketing at the time consisted mostly of the pop-up street displays Norman had built and posters with the legendary tagline "cocaine is so 80s." Posters with that tagline were hot commodities, and they didn't last very long on the walls of pubs and construction sites, especially in Berlin.

He also set up our in-house graphic design department. The sales guys affectionately called the marketing team "the crayons" because they were always in such a good mood, and they got to play with pretty pictures instead of dull Excel spreadsheets. Event-based marketing, referring to how we'd set up refrigerated trailers and mobile bars at festivals and other such occasions, was another focus in that period.

But most of the ad work is directed at our customers generating the most revenue — bars, restaurants, and food retailers — and supporting their own in-house sales efforts. This entails launching campaigns of our own in each city and region. We tailor these efforts to the location in question and use allusions that would only make sense and amuse the people who actually live there. Here are a few examples of such ads in Munich.

brand management à la fritz

Our marketing was very successful back then — it seemed we could do no wrong. Patrick took the lead of the newly established Brand Management department. When he left us in 2012, his replacement was fortunately already in the company: Jana Hollenberg had begun doing internal sales with us in September 2011. She was 25 at the time, and she had a fresh marketing and communication diploma in her pocket. Her degree didn't suit the job description perfectly, but she made it clear to us in the interview that she was willing to do any job to get her foot in the door at such an exciting brand. As the contact person for the road sales crew in the southwest region, she had been diligently ordering fritz refrigerators and illuminated fluorescent ad boards for our hospitality customers in addition to organizing trade shows and sales meetings. When Patrick left, we were pleased to see that she didn't hesitate for a second before taking on the leadership position we offered her. It was clear to both sides that we were taking a leap of faith. A 26-year-old, who'd only been working with us for a year and who didn't have the least experience in marketing, was supposed to take responsibility for our brand image, communicate our brand, and oversee a small

team. But if an entrepreneur wants to revitalize things, they have to be brave and sometimes take risks, which will be richly rewarded when they succeed. We believed in Jana because she fit the fritz team perfectly and reflected our team spirit. That might have been iffy with a polished professional from outside. Later, after we had grown and become complacent in our "us-against-the-world" routine, we might have taken the opposite approach, reasoning that we desperately needed fresh blood from outside, and if the candidate didn't tick like a veteran fritz, more's the better. Sometimes when team members get too comfortable with each other, they need to be woken up a bit.

Jana explains the first steps she took:

By the time I got started, the two founders and Patrick Keller had already achieved the first milestones and secured some brand recognition. I didn't doubt their potential for a second; I had fallen in love with the underdog brand from Hamburg while I was still in college. The patience, courage, and the gut feeling that I got from Mirco and Lorenz, which was almost always positive, paid off with several other projects and campaigns during my time at fritz. I'll never forget the first national billboard campaign in 2013 with the bottle-cap motif, "tired? — awake!" from the creative duo of Rocket & Wink.

The brand and the agency cleaned up at the creativity awards with that campaign, including the famous Best-18/1-Award and the ADC (Art Directors Club) prize. Boy, were we proud!

Christening the first fritz-kola city bus was also great. We and the "crayon" team took a field trip to the Hamburg public transport depot, and we were among the first passengers in the black-and-white caffeine transporter.

When I worked there, my team reported to Lorenz, who was the director responsible for marketing. During a meeting with the Hamburg Society for the Arts, the opportunity came up at short notice to use the highly visible façade of their building for a huge, high-profile billboard in an unbeatable location. Lorenz didn't need to be told twice! We needed to come up with a motif for the oversized spot quickly. We opted for a little fritz unicorn, which Rocket & Wink had originally designed only for use on t-shirts; we adapted it rapidly for the new huge size, and it went on to become a favorite among fritz fans. We followed it up with t-shirts, stickers, and stuffed animals. A new fritz motif shows up in that spot regularly to this day, and I always keep an eye out for it when I roll into Hamburg on the train. It's still a great deal!

My time at fritz-kola will probably always remain the most influential of my career, with so many highs and lows, priceless moments, countless wins, and sleepless nights. And

the friendships I made at fritz connect me to the brand to this day.

Setting up a department for brand management was both necessary and sensible. Of course, we continue to work enthusiastically and successfully with agencies. But you should never completely delegate and outsource the work on your own brand's identity. You will always need in-house people to develop original ideas, to coordinate with the agencies, and especially to ensure that the brand's image doesn't become disconnected from developments in the market and the company. And that's impossible to determine without sitting in the head office with constant contact to the customers.

Our campaigns regularly turn heads, and beyond yielding some nice revenue boosts, they're a lot of fun for us too. Basically, all of our campaigns revolve around the idea of "being awake," emphasizing the caffeine content of our kola. Examples include "at least you're awake" (*hauptsache wach*) and "welcome to the wake up" (*willkommen im wach*), which both appear in several variations.

We always considered the caffeine content to be *the* unique characteristic of our product, and the taste-test party that raged until ten a. m. confirmed it. Awake also means "mentally present" to us. This relates to our

involvement in social issues and the wokeness of our target market. Since late 2019 we've printed the bottom of our restaurant bottles with a credo: "The world belongs to the woke." Being awake and woke means paying attention, taking responsibility, taking a stand, and questioning prevailing conditions rather than taking them for granted.

One occurrence that attracted plenty of attention in Hamburg was "the sea monster," a giant kola-kraken floating on the Elbe River. In the fall of 2014, we managed to book the ridiculously long exterior wall of the Blohm & Voss Shipyard on dock 11. For those unfamiliar with Hamburg, that dock is right in the middle of the harbor,

directly across from the St. Pauli Piers — one of the city's most renowned landmarks — and it's probably the best and most visible advertising space in town. As with everything seen across a body of water, the view is never obscured. As a Hamburg business, we wanted to be present in that space at least once no matter what, and we got our chance to cover the 1,700 square meters with our motif in 2014. It cost a mint, of course.

We booked a harbor tour for our entire staff when the sea monster was unveiled to give all our people a front-row seat right under the gigantic image. Many jaws dropped, both because the billboard was so breath-takingly enormous and because our "little" kola from Hamburg managed to do something so huge. Because that's still how we felt: like the little guy mixing it up with the giants. We commissioned the artist Robert Matzke, aka Rookie the Weird, for that billboard. Afterwards, we had the huge, printed plastic sheet turned into tote bags.

Looking back, I think we missed an opportunity there. We had discussed at length how provocative the motif should be. It still bothers me that I pushed for the less aggressive version at the time instead of something that would have gotten under the skin of our counterparts in red and white. At the end of the day, we spent a lot of money on little impact, even though the fritzes remember it so fondly. It's not uncommon for painstakingly prepared ad campaigns and corporate promotional videos to have a largely internal effect and only an ephemeral public impact. To prevent a skewed perspective, it's necessary to have people from the outside who can share their external perspectives and dispel the ideas developed internally, which are often too complicated. What the audience out there take from the message is what counts, not what the company's management intends.

The city buses driving around Hamburg as fritz's brand ambassadors also attracted plenty of attention. As many as seven branded, black "monstrosities" were crawling through the port city — an uber-conspicuous mode of advertising for our *limo*, *spritz*, and *mischmasch* products. We later refocused on fritz-kola and reduced the number of buses. In 2020 we were down to a single big, black fritz-kola bus that's employed all around the city.

This mode of advertising was and remains relatively cheap, but it's impossible to tell whether it's really working and generating value — these considerations are indispensable in my view. Advertising must increase sales, revenue, recognition, or popularity.

People sometimes ask me whether fritz-kola is a "cult favorite." I have no time for that term. Words like

"cult favorite," "hipster," and "trendy" are banned in our offices because they're utter nonsense. It's a different story if fans, clients, or consumers use such labels to describe us, in which case they can be badges of honor. But companies should avoid hollow terms. You can't say, "now we're going *cult*." You can do things, like make a good soft drink with a good design. You do it because you think it's the right thing to do. And then others can come and say, "I dig this," but we don't actively use such terms.

For a long time, we at fritz joked that we were out to achieve "world domination." At first, it was inconceivable to us that anyone outside our immediate range, a radius of maybe 250 or 300 miles, would want to drink fritz-kola. The horizon of our activity and imagination was limited by the distance we could cover in our used cars. My old

VW van in particular wasn't suitable for long distances. That's why I covered northern and eastern Germany, while Lorenz covered southern and western Germany in his VW Golf, which was still in good condition. Soon, though, we were receiving inquiries from Amsterdam, Barcelona, Copenhagen, Vienna, Warsaw, and other locations in Europe and beyond. The significance of being an alternative cola brand slowly started to dawn on us. Why shouldn't we be selling to bars, cafés, and clubs beyond the range of our jalopies? A real indie kola with lots-n-lots of caffeine, sold in reusable glass bottles, can wake people anywhere.

Therefore, we began to expand our network of European cities. On our travels, I started to notice how much the range of beverages changed from one language region to the next and that only a few brands were present throughout all or even most of Europe. At first, I had no idea why this would be the case. After a number of discussions though, I grasped that many of us Europeans like to travel from one end of the continent to the other, but on an average day we don't think or work beyond our national borders. As a result, I'm even more pleased that we've managed to create a real European fritz-kola network in the last few years, which is becoming ever more European itself. In effect, many Europeans identify

with both the continent and their own nation. We can now help people in several cities across the continent to burn the midnight oil, to get a nice caffeine buzz, and to enjoy a cool refreshment along with a paella or a pizza.

It's still exciting to see how fritz-kola is making its way in the world. A restaurateur might see one of our bottles somewhere, either in real life or online on one of countless platforms, and then they'll contact us. Such inquiries typically come from bars, cafés, pubs, and nightspots in the more liberal and alternative neighborhoods of major cities. Sometimes they come from beach bars that want to transition from disposable to reusable packaging or cultural institutions looking for alternatives to Big Corporate. Sometimes they just come from people opening a new place nowhere in particular, off the beaten path, who are thinking about what to include on the menu. Some of those who discover us also inspire their local distributors to list us.

At that point, we'll help them to arrange reliable deliveries, which can provide a number of people with their first contact to fritz-kola. It sounds simple at first — even romantic. It's totally analog and maybe even a little antiquated, but that's how it has worked. Not only does it help our revenue, it also helps many people earn a living.

From experience, I recommend to all founders: <mark>Do your absolute best to serve the customers you have! Put all your time, care, and passion into it!</mark> Make sure that they look forward to working with you, enjoy the process, and happily tell others about it. Good work leads to good references, and that's how you get new customers. Reflect on what distinguishes you from others. Your service and your charm should be selling points — not just your product.

Coca-Cola really began to take us seriously once we introduced the 200 ml bottle in 2005.

mirco wolf wiegert

Of course, we don't operate fritz-kola in a vacuum. The market environment was pretty comfortable when we began: there was a somewhat complacent monopolist, and the range of soft drink and colas available was pathetic. Both have since changed fundamentally. The market for non-alcoholic beverages is now vibrant and vital. Each year sees new soft drinks and other similar beverages joining the market. Only a fraction will manage to become established brands and to hold their own. Once upon a time, it was enough to fill a tasty drink into a bottle somehow, but today's market entrants face much higher expectations. The requirements from day one now include:

- A coherent idea and a clear answer to the question of why the beverage is good and sensible
- A clear approach to the four Ps: which product are we going to sell at what price with what kind of promotion and in which place, and how are we going to distribute it?
- An appealing design — clear, self-explanatory, and eye-catching
- High quality — the market is becoming ever-less forgiving

- A smoothly functioning reorder system to prevent customers from having empty inventories
- Communication channels, especially online
- A sustainable packaging solution, ideally with access to a pool of reusable crates and bottles
- A team with marathon-grade endurance.

Playing the beverage game for a relatively long time has made us more professional. In 2020 Nielsen Market Research rated us the number three cola brand in Germany. In practice, that means we have a market share of two percent, excluding discount stores and drug stores. No comparable data from the hospitality industry is collected.

Whether the metaphor of the little David from Hamburg versus Big Corporate still applies is a matter of perspective. The fritz era has provided many people with lots of fun and an income, though it has probably cost them a few tears as well.

As we've become more popular, we've naturally attracted more attention. The brownie points we enjoyed for being the underdog have dissipated. The big guys have us on their radar now, which is both a source of pride and aggravation. For example, it's frustrating when colossal competitors release new varieties that strongly resemble our own products and those of other, even smaller craft-soda producers. But it's also flattering when someone imitates our advertising materials, or their branding suddenly goes monochromatic despite their usual palette being based on red. But it can drive us crazy when such materials replace fritz-kola billboards and street displays, erasing our presence from the street. We really start to sweat when they start targeted, blanket campaigns to convince our hospitality customers to either delist us or include us only as a secondary brand, no longer as their primary or exclusive choice.

Another move in some major competitors' repertoire is to crowd fritz out of the supermarket shelves by expanding their own bloated product ranges. This includes swamping the purchasers of supermarket chains with planograms for their beverage departments, showing how an optimal arrangement of the department would look in their estimation. Smaller producers, like fritz-kola, wind up on the bottom shelves, if they're included at all. And don't forget the PowerPoint battles emphasizing the advantages of the sales rep's own brand relative to their competitors.

A report in the Berlin newspaper *Tagesspiegel*, which tracks another cola's sales rep through the Friedrichshain

district of Berlin, demonstrates that all is fair in love and market share. It talks about how much better the other cola operates and how fritz-kola is being repelled. Looking at one of our ads, the rep is quoted as saying, "Frankly, I don't get this ad at all." Tools like "statistics, big data, and complex, mobile market analyses," help her do her job, along with "proven, old-fashioned sales tactics, like visiting with the customers, going door to door, and not taking no for an answer. Any restaurateur who sends her away is sure to see her again before long." Two photos show her with smiling restaurateurs, happily selling the rep's brand of cola and having already emptied another, smaller soft drink brand out of the refrigerator — all ready to be picked up after being delisted. That article showed me how far we've actually come. It gave me goosebumps.

One positive aspect of this struggle for the affections of customers and fans is that we've managed to increase the acceptance of reusable bottles in the category of indie-kolas, soft drinks, and spritzers. Even our larger competitors are increasingly using reusable packaging and phasing out disposables. Moreover, customers have definitely become more aware of things like the quality of the ingredients and the finished product. Artificial flavors and colors have become less common and are typically only found in imported canned beverages. As far as I know, no other European country enjoys this tempting treat in such high quality. It all goes to show that the market we're in is no hug-a-thon, and we're being taken seriously.

Based on the experience I've gathered in recent years, I remind anyone thinking about going out on their own and being self-employed that others will not sit idly by and watch you succeed. Try to stay fair and continue your journey with passion, even if others play rough. At fritz, we ask ourselves fundamental questions each year: Who are we? What's unique about us? Where is there untapped potential? Where do we need to improve? What might be out of date? And what does it mean for fritz-kola if the game gets even rougher and others imitate us? Such external pressure can be really draining, but it keeps us awake and alert.

In practice, this could mean calling up customers we've lost and asking them why they've decided against us. In the best case, they'll send the entire presentation deck that they received from the other cola and that led to their change of heart, which can reveal things like how our own product was trashed using all available means. What a gift! Through discoveries of that kind, we've learned how to better highlight our strengths and how to systematically mitigate our weaknesses. Sometimes all that's needed is to improve our own communication. For example, we learned that another big cola's sales reps were spreading the rumor that our kola wasn't being produced in Germany, but instead was imported from Eastern Europe. As a result, we started to improve our messaging about our decentralized, local production. (The instrumentalization and promotion of prejudicial attitudes toward Eastern Europe is typical of such sales tactics and completely beyond the pale of decency.)

We've learned never to speak negatively about the competition when addressing third parties. That should obviously be the norm — you'd think.

A friend who owns a bar in St. Pauli likes to tell the story of how his Coca-Cola sales rep once showed up to an appointment with his new regional manager. The regional manager immediately started tearing into fritz-kola, without noticing the awkward silence descending around the table. The sales rep finally stopped him and explained that the bar owner and Lorenz were very good friends. The regional manager piped up again meekly and tried to backpedal out of his faux pas. The bar owner generously suggested that everyone forget the previous two minutes, and they start all over again. He's also told us that Coca-Cola occasionally offers him perverse discounts should he agree to delist us. One 2020 publication of theirs indicated how we're getting under their skin: it listed all competing brands by name, except fritz-kola.

A certain anti-Big-Corporate attitude in some circles definitely helped us to be initially perceived as an attractive alternative on the market and to achieve a given scale. But attitudes can change. We've managed to build momentum and win people over with our quality and taste, building a brand identity that doesn't depend on current events or ephemeral fluctuations in public attitudes.

Inspirations and Imitations

Bionade was a ready-made inspiration for us. They had been in business for eight years already when we got started in 2003, but they only really became established in the market around the time that we did. We'd often meet at industry events, and we worked well together in such situations, as when we'd meet customers who were open to smaller indie brands and wanted to expand their product portfolio. We would recommend each other. Our palettes complemented each other well, especially in the early days, and we played off each other for a while. I've always thought that they had a good story — a brewery about to go under that completely reinvented itself and pulled itself out of the quicksand by its own bootstraps. Bionade had deeply penetrated the restaurant business, which was an inspiration we modeled ourselves after. Their product palette and presentation were stripped down to the bare essentials. And the first generation of their staff was comprised of true believers in the cause.

Premium Cola was launched about six months before fritz-kola, and Uwe Lübbermann, the founder, approached us in Hamburg's China Lounge soon after we had started. Uwe wanted to touch base with a couple of kindred spirits, and he was desperate to get his hands on the lost original recipe for Afri-Cola, which had disappeared from the market, combined with lots of caffeine. And he started out with the pitch that Premium-Cola was reviving that flavor that he missed so dearly. Afri-Cola later forbade him from using that line. Nowadays, they identify as "the Premium Collective," which they define as "basically everyone who's involved in any way: producers, shippers, retailers, restaurateurs, and especially consumers. To anyone who's ever drunk a bottle, we welcome him/her/them to read up and share his/her/their voice in contribution." It's a really interesting project because Uwe is trying to rethink and reorganize the business aspects from the ground up. The remote company is led by a sort of collective, in which employees can determine their own work hours, and they all receive a uniform salary. They dispense with classical hierarchies. Uwe and his powerhouse crew want to show everyone that a different, more humane mode of capital-ism than what is currently practiced is possible. The pro-duct they happen to use to demonstrate this is more of an afterthought for them. I greatly respect the courage and determination that the people at Premium have displayed for more than twenty years.

In 2004 word of our success was getting around, and we first saw others trying to jump on the bandwagon. That's fine, as long as there's no infringement. "Peace Cola — drink it for peace" was not an infringement. The founders were profiting from the same political climate as we were. That cola was only around for about a year, and I sadly never got to meet the founder, Jens Marsau.

But we've also had to deal regularly with wannabes who take inspiration from our success without coming up with a genuinely new product idea of their own. At first, that sort of thing upset us, but we've since grown more chilled about it. Whenever something pops up trying to be like fritz, customers simply prefer the original.

The first time we encountered this problem was in 2009, when our bottler in North Rhine-Westphalia was having trouble producing fritz-kola in consistently good quality. When we switched bottlers, the jilted master brewer was so upset that he spoke to a neighbor who was on his way up to Hamburg to start college. Would he perhaps have any interest in selling a new cola up in the big city? I first took notice of that brand when I was

walking past a bakery in the Grindel district, and I was pleased to see out of the corner of my eye that they were selling our kola. On closer inspection, it turned out to be the new cola after all. It was monochrome, just like us, it bore the slogan "boosted caffeine content," and it showed the silhouette of a person instead of our two heads. A coffee-flavored cola — to all appearances a fritz — but it never got anywhere.

Our exclusive distributor in North Rhine-Westphalia was much more shameless about it. He supplied and managed the accounts of all fritz's customers in the most populous state in Germany, so he was an important partner. He surprised us with the launch of his own cola in 2006. It had a monochrome label — of course. And he was wildly innovative with the name: an old-fashioned man's name. When we asked him what he thought he was doing, he replied that we could compete against each other like Coke and Pepsi.

There was little we could do legally against this breach of trust. Our kola had helped him gain access to our customers, and now he was trying to convince them to order his own brand instead of fritz. The way he presented the undertaking on his company's homepage was also a thorn in our side. He claimed to be trans- forming the family business, shifting it to specialize in "alternative refreshments and beverages" and "to gain independence from the major brands and the supposedly alternative, independent beverage producers." It hurt to watch as he reverse-engineered our entire palette product by product, copying us as exactly as possible while calling us "supposedly alternative." We rescinded his exclusivity deal for North Rhine-Westphalia, and from then on, we sold directly to other distributors in the region. Luckily, we managed to limit the damage and to continue supplying nearly all of our customers in the hospitality industry there with fritz-kola. We did have to resume the account management activities there ourselves.

The lesson from this shameless imitation is obvious: it's not enough to just bottle a kola and package it like a company riding an earlier wave. Like most consumer goods, a kola needs a unique identity. That was the flaw. Simply copying something successful might work in the short term, but it's neither clever nor sustainable.

Losing our distributor in Poland, BioBox, was another serious blow. They had been supplying and managing the accounts of our Polish customers, including hospitality and food retail, since 2011. They launched a mate drink of their own in that same year, but fritz remained their biggest seller by far in the cola and soft drink segment.

In 2014 they unexpectedly launched a soft drink line of their own called John Lemon, and they informed us that they planned to offer their own brand in competition with fritz. We terminated the deal that very day and were left scratching our heads. We had to placate our customers while desperately searching for new partners who would deliver to them. The newly renamed John Lemon company conquered nearly the entire Polish market for a while, and one of their flagships was a John Lemon kola that contained exactly 25 mg of caffeine. What a coincidence. We also couldn't help noticing how all of our advertising materials and monochrome refrigerators were copied exactly.

During that time, we lost droves of customers and loads of revenue in Poland, which we only managed to regain after reinvesting considerable time and effort. Amusingly enough, John Lemon's legal troubles weren't with us, but with Yoko Ono. She successfully sued against the use of a name that resembled her murdered husband's too closely. The company then renamed itself ON Lemon. ON Lemon released some good, innovative products with a distinct profile, like the line of tonic waters they launched in 2019. We can learn a lot from them. Those guys have built their own identity over the years, and they do good business in Poland alongside us. But the loss of BioBox still hurts because they were a really good and congenial team. We could have achieved much more together, but we also had a great run together in Poland. Although the affair cost us plenty of time and money, we're once again an integral part of the Polish hospitality scene thanks to our dedicated staff in Poland.

Three conclusions can be drawn from these affairs with our old business partners and shameless copycats. First, we're now much less naïve in choosing whom to cooperate with and in structuring the interaction. Second, the contracts keep getting thicker. Third, it's unfortunately the case that even the thickest contracts cannot prevent all abuse. Once a process is already underway, no contract can stop it. It's just like in professional soccer: if a player is determined to go to another club, he'll do so regardless of what his contract may say.

Either way, it's important to consider how much energy to invest in legal battles. The old lawyers' saying that "In court and on the high seas, you're in God's hands" shows that the outcome of a legal dispute is hard to predict. But such confrontations definitely do consume massive amounts of money, time, energy, and goodwill. And they can also cost you your good image in

the customers' eyes, even if not only the law is on your side, but justice too. Sometimes, the wiser course of action is to give in at some point and to invest the resources in projects that are more fun and have good prospects.

Sometimes trademark-related questions arise from interactions with the public, as was the case with a craft beer called "FritzAle." Fritz Wülfing, a brewer from Bonn, released that beer in 2010, simply naming it after himself.

But people kept asking us about "our beer." We were still inexperienced in dealing with questions of trademark, so in 2012 we asked our lawyer to take care of it, which he then did. He sent a letter, written in impeccable legalese, asking the FritzAle brand to cease and desist. The beer was confusing people, and fritz-kola brand antedated it, so we were on the right side of the law. Looking back, though, it was the wrong way to go about things. It was bad form. We first should have tried to settle the matter without lawyers. Fritz Wülfing is a decent guy, and he surely would have been amenable.

We subsequently experienced how the public instinctively takes the side of the underdog, and we learned that we weren't the underdog anymore. Instead, many perceived us as the hard-hearted, capitalist corporation that had forgotten where it came from. Few people stopped to consider that using the name Fritz, which we had established, was not a very smart move for a beer. We then reversed course and reached an out-of-court settlement with Fritz Wülfing — in which the shitstorm raining down on us played no small role — according to which he could continue selling his remaining FritzAle inventory for a few months before choosing a new name for his product: Ale-Mania. It's still a really great beer.

We learned a lot from that experience. Compared to the rookies, we had become the Big Guys — the Establishment — which didn't fit very well with our still-beloved self-image of "David." Before starting a lawsuit, it's important to consider what impact it could have on a company's image and not to give too much credence to the lawyers and the bare facts of the matter. Public sentiment is an important factor, and it's easy to misjudge from inside your bubble. It's natural to feel that you're in the right. You might even actually be in the right, but will your fans see it that way too? And is it going to suit your brand's valuable image and reputation if you go around siccing lawyers on everyone? Whenever possible, try to settle with competitors and imitators amiably, silently, and out of court. We learned that the hard way.

Ever since the FritzAle affair, we first call or meet people who are launching products that are too similar to ours. That's how we convinced Aydin Umutlu, who was releasing "Ali-Cola," that a cola with a monochrome label and Ali's head on it was a doomed undertaking. People would always be confusing those bottles with fritz-kola, and he'd never be able to build his own customer base or a unique identity. He then came up with the very original idea of forgoing big labels entirely and letting his cola, which was available in six different colors, speak for itself. In his advertising, he used taglines that called for tolerance, like "Do people have to be white and colas black? I know, right!?" and "Cola has always been skin-colored, just not *your* skin." We've met a few times since. Cool guy. Great idea.

We again found ourselves in the role of the heartless Goliath in 2015. The first calls to reach us were a shock: "Oh, crap. *DIE ZEIT*, the national newspaper, is shredding you in the lead story of its college magazine with several pages of detailed, full-color graphics. Daaamn!"

What was happening? A guy who owned a snack bar located in a supermarket parking lot down in the Ruhr valley rust belt was of the opinion that we were trying to crowd out the little, local "Ruhr-Pott-Kohla" with our expensive advertising materials, like benches, umbrellas, and refrigerators. *Campus* magazine ran with that story and used it as an occasion to criticize us for crowding smaller competitors out of bars and restaurants or just buying them out. In cooperation with a local Hamburg magazine, we organized a roundtable including fritz-kola, Premium Cola, Ali-Cola, Cola-Rebell, and Ruhr-Pott-Kohla, all of whom were present or participating online. I requested that all criticism be accompanied by concrete examples. Nobody could come up with any aside from a

story from our early days, when one of our sales reps had tried to have a competitor delisted from a club with inappropriate offers of free product, which we immediately and permanently forbade.

One old and continuing practice is for some restaurateurs to sell placement on their drink menus, or they'll take a cut for exclusive deals on individual beverage categories, like non-alcoholic beverages, beers, waters, juices, energy drinks, and spirits, from beverage producers. They use the money to print new menus or to invest in their place. Especially for music clubs and live-music locations, this is a standard part of the business model that allows them to operate and stay open. We also participate in this market to a certain degree and share a portion of our margin with the outlets if we can.

While this practice does represent a significant hurdle for smaller beverage producers, it's also important to understand the predicament of those who own and enjoy great music clubs. As cities become more expensive, with prices for rent and labor constantly rising, they use money and support from breweries, distilleries, and tobacco companies to refinance themselves. This is standard practice in expensive urban areas, but it's somewhat rarer in cheaper and more alternative places. In the latter, the operators tend to have more space and financial latitude to try out new ideas and pay for them on their own (until the COVID-induced, industry-wide crisis). Alternatively, new operators can also now obtain financing from outside investors. In the 2020s, money in the bank doesn't earn interest anymore, so investment capital flows more easily into — usually upper-class — hospitality businesses, which allows them to do without money from the beverage industry.

This phenomenon is especially prevalent at music festivals. The promoter agencies have to juggle the rising demands of the musicians and artists, who depend on the live-performance fees and ticket sales for their income, the diverse risks associated with live events, local regulations, and compensating their own work. Sponsors, like telecom firms, supermarket chains, and, yes, beverage producers are a welcome, additional source of revenue. The effects of the COVID crisis, which has hit the hospitality, club, and festival scene extremely hard, had not yet played out by the publication deadline of this book.

We support a functioning ecosystem of independent, generally small beverage producers as a basic principle. After all, one inspiration for founding fritz-kola was the lack of selection in the beverage market. The smaller producers tend to know each other, and they try to learn from each other with more or less success.

As far as further colas go, I'm of the opinion that we've reached the end of the road for now. There are Coca-Cola and Pepsi, there are the house brands, and there are several independent brands like fritz. Naturally, they all have a huge head start over potential entrants. Successfully penetrating this market would now be unthinkable without some spectacular innovation. But what would that be? When we started, we found an uncultivated, fertile field before us, but restaurateurs can no longer keep up with trying all the sample bottles of new colas and other soft drinks they're being sent. There's simply no way; there are just too many.

growth spurts and growing pains

The early days were characterized by the typical startup atmosphere, where everybody did everything, and everyone could rely on others' help when the going got tough. The organization is now much more professional, but also less wacky and funny. The scale is just lots-n-lots bigger than it used to be.

rabea haase, bookkeeper since 2010

At some point after those wild early years, we could no longer deny that we had become a real enterprise with offices, departments, internal structures, office equipment worthy of the name, and even insurance policies for the most expensive parts of it (computers and servers). Still, we managed the growth process with a lean team for a surprisingly long time. It was only after about a decade — around 2014 — that our staff started to grow into its current dimensions.

Nor was there any denying our furious growth, which hovered around 30–50 percent for several years. I have often been asked whether the ever-rising figures and the ever-expanding horizons of possibility that our fritz-kola project has achieved have ever made me dizzy. But even though I was shocked to realize that I was going to be giving a speech to almost 200 people at our Christmas party one year (a number we have since surpassed), our success has never been much of an enigma. From the very beginning, Lorenz and I were audacious enough to envision our project in grossly outsized dimensions. And our vision has kept pace with actual growth, always staying ahead of the real numbers. The cause was our unshakable conviction in our idea and its market potential. Looking back, I would say that I have pursued my goal of becoming an entrepreneur with single-minded determination, without ever considering the possibility of failure. I would have tackled any obstacle in my way, even if it were three meters high.

But we were still just the two kids from the utility room, who were running their business according to their income and bank balance instead of solid key performance indicators. Our principal performance indicator was our bank balance at the Hamburger Sparkasse. If one month's balance was higher than the last, that was good; if it was lower, well, then that was bad and needed to be changed. It was cut and dried. We didn't have any complicated analyses, tools, or even the time to pause, reflect, and adjust. We were too busy with our own growth. We learned a lot, and we made many mistakes. But the business was going so well that we didn't notice.

I have since learned that we absolutely should have devoted some time each year to reflection and proper planning, ideally with the input of external experts, like mentors or a board of experienced advisors. As much as sheer will originally helped us to unleash our venture's potential with our own means, it gradually became a weakness as our scale increased. We simply lacked the right toolbox and the experience to lead and expand an enterprise as large as we had become.

In many ways, it's easier when a company is growing rapidly. The mistakes you inevitably make that cost you revenue or cash in hand are not existential threats because the rapid growth conceals and swallows their effects. That's exactly why the overall economic malaise that followed the 2008 financial crisis left no visible trace on our balance sheet: we were already experiencing a period of extraordinary growth. Our annual gains were far larger than the losses resulting from the macro-economic situation, so the former rendered the latter invisible.

At the same time, furious growth is also challenging because the business's structures require constant adjustment. As an entrepreneur, you often feel like the parent of a teenager who's growing six inches each year. You have to be constantly adapting yourself to this process. You're perpetually buying new clothes and shoes, a new bed, a new desk, and a new bike. In our case, that meant more new people, new spaces, and a constant stream of questions that had never even occurred to us. Sure, those are great problems to have, but they still keep management and the staff on their toes. Constantly hurtling forward also means never taking a break. And you have to safeguard yourself against recklessness and overconfidence, which is a policy that's much easier to justify to employees in times of unmistakable crisis than in times of plenty.

But is such constant growth even necessary or desirable in the first place? Why should fritz-kola keep growing? When we founded the company, the point was simply for two college students to earn a living and to "do their thing" independently. The end of that phase was soon in coming. The students' lives and their business were growing up fast. The urgency of those crazy first years has passed. Anyone questioning the bigger meaning behind why fritz should continue to grow will quickly wind up back at the fifth P: purpose. Why are we doing this anyway? My answer: with success and growth come the power to effect change. Increased resources and responsibility are the consequences of success and growth. Using them for the good of the business and of the society of which it is a part is the reason we want to grow. In recent years, we've been able to watch how other founders, both men and women, have taken inspiration from our success to invest time and money in sustainable projects.

If we maintain fritz's growth, we'll be able to provide more incentives for farmers to make the transition to organic agriculture. We'll expand the market for organically grown produce and we'll raise consumers'

awareness. Organic farming protects the planet's bio-diversity, and it raises and maintains the soil's fecundity without the use of chemicals. Done right, it can provide a decent income for generations of people around the world. That's what makes our effort to buy more organic products and to supply our growing fandom with kola, soft drinks, and spritzers worthwhile.

Our success in recent years has encouraged other beverage producers to follow our lead, to take the plunge with reusable containers, and to ditch disposables. Reusables enable regional bottlers to prosper in spite of disposable factories that flood the world with their cheap sugar water gushing from a central plant across hundreds and thousands of miles. Our approach is a real and sustainable alternative. Instead of winding up as garbage on the outskirts of the city, in rivers and oceans, in Europe and overseas, reusable bottles get fed back into the local circular economy. Shortening transportation routes helps in the fight against climate change and fosters the local economy, which is good for both employment rates and tax revenues. The droves of beverage producers that have adopted sustainable production practices have recently led many consumers to appreciate the value of reusables.

Successful brands like fritz-kola enable investment in sustainability thanks to stable, long-term partnerships. The success of the one is what makes the other's investment in new, future-oriented plants possible. More often than not, it's local, family-run enterprises, like that of Dirk Lütvogt, whose investments we're helping to enable.

Our aim as fritz-kola to "stay awake together," to inspire people everywhere to "do their thing," and to get involved for the sake of an open, liberal society can serve as our motivation never to stop working to make the best kola.

In 2008 our growth meant that it was time for us to look for a new space. Until then, we had been using an old shed on the outskirts of town as a warehouse, and we'd been renting a dingy storefront on a trunk road. The

time had come for something bigger and for everything to be united under one roof. We got lucky when we found an old Colgate-Palmolive factory that was available in the Billbrook district of Hamburg, affectionally called "Billbrooklyn," long before numerous food startups moved into the area.

Jana Hollenberg, our marketing lead (at fritz, we say "Brand Management Lead"), remembers the atmosphere at our new headquarters:

The first time I encountered fritz-kola was at my job interview in the summer of 2011 in the old fritz offices in Hamburg-Billbrook(lyn). The journey to that remote industrial area on Hamburg's east side was a bit of an adventure in itself, and it was the first step of my initiation. The offices were hidden on the disused premises of the Colgate-Palmolive facility; the elevator got stuck so often that it was more of a human-sized trap, and the entrance with its tiny logo was hard to spot between a trucking academy and some other, rather dubious import-export outfits. Fortunately, I didn't let that intimidate me, and I signed my contract only two weeks later. Lorenz, who was wearing a cap, hoodie, and sneakers when he greeted me before the interview, quickly won me over and convinced me to join the yet-small fritz team.

The work environment in the Liebig St. offices was pretty odd, and not only because of our neighbors' dubious businesses. Thanks to the poor insulation, the building could get a little frosty in the winter. But the superintendent had a quick and pragmatic solution — he simply sealed the window frames with Scotch tape. That didn't help much of course, but we put a brave face on it — and wore a warm hat.

When I started at fritz, there were only about two dozen of us, with around ten in the Hamburg offices. But the staff then grew furiously. We quickly grew into other rooms on that floor, picking up and assembling the new Ikea office furniture ourselves, with the more handy among us helping the others. Speed was the main thing. All hands would also help to put together the promotional packs with bottle openers, glasses, and key fobs down in the warehouse, which was then in the same building. New employees were soon hired for that purpose, but shipping promotional materials was eventually outsourced. It also became increasingly difficult to remember the names of all the new sales reps spread across Germany. While we started using only first names for email addresses, we soon had to supplement them with last names, and we'd have to book hotels and conference rooms for sales meetings far in advance. Each "class reunion" with new fritz faces would cause plenty of astonishment at the kickoff, and the two founders were no exception. Those moments probably brought home to them the most how their little startup team had grown into a medium-sized enterprise.

world domination à la fritz

From the beginning, our so-called "caffex" (caffeine experts) sales reps were the core of fritz. We completely embraced Peter Thiele's motto that "startups need to make selling their product the top priority, not production. You can outsource production." It wouldn't be an exaggeration to say that fritz was really all about sales in the first few years. All other tasks were either outsourced to ad agencies or accounting firms, for example, or handled by the in-office sales staff.

Our team of sales reps eventually grew so large that we no longer held general sales meetings in Hamburg, but instead in more central locations with more space. The first was in 2007 in Weimar. These meetings have always been among the high points in each fritz year. We celebrate our successes and plan how to achieve new ones.

There has been much to celebrate. The constant expansion of our activities demonstrates our growth. We're constantly penetrating new cities, regions, and countries, gaining new customer segments — like food retail — and regularly expanding our product line. What our caffexes might have lacked in experience, they've more than made up for with motivation. With targeted precision, they have established contacts with women and men in modern, attractive hospitality businesses. With remarkable endurance and commitment, they have filled the shelves of independent retailers with our products, even as others would now and then replace our bottles with those of our competition. Our displays, consisting of crates and bottles arranged between the supermarket aisles in the shape of, say, a soccer arena while a championship is underway, a heart on Valentine's Day, or a locomotive in a shop near a rail museum, are legendary. Our people have always been the cornerstone of the successes we celebrate.

We exported our first shipment in 2005, although we never really made any kind of sharp distinction between domestic and foreign. Whoever wants fritz-kola is our customer. Period. And the common market in Europe is a blessing in that it spares us the trouble of having to worry very much about national particularities and regulations.

The first such new customer was the "TROUW Club" in Amsterdam, which succeeded the legendary "Club 11" and was already a legend itself in the world of electronic music. Austria, Switzerland, and Spain followed in 2006, and then Poland and Denmark in 2010 — always hot on the trail of the most exciting cafés, bars, and clubs. We

also met Florian Frey and Azadeh Falashahi at the 2010 Internorga hospitality trade show. They were in the process of opening the first of their sausage joints called "Herman ze German" in London, and fritz-kola fit the bill precisely. And for me it was a perfect reason to travel to London, the hyper-hip heart of what was then admiringly called "Cool Britannia." Azadeh remembers:

When we encountered fritz-kola, we were totally enthusiastic about the idea, the language, the brand, and the team. About the visions and the message. The team lived by a refreshing code. The branding language fritz-kola uses is ingenious. They always have the best and bravest taglines and images. And the drinks are totally delicious. Our customers love the brand and the flavor.

We identified immediately with Mirco's enthusiasm and stamina. And we've always had lots of fun with the guys on their occasional visits to London. We found it strange that Mirco insisted on walking everywhere. It was also always a blast to translate the tagline "cocaine is so 1980s" (koksen ist achtziger) for the Londoners.

At first, we'd import entire pallets of fritz-kola ourselves because there weren't any distributors yet. Our place was full of the black crates. We couldn't afford to run out. Today we have five outlets selling fritz-kola products almost exclusively.

We gradually won over new customer segments. The family-owned Budnikowsky chain of drugstores, which is a local institution in Hamburg and is referred to by the locals as "Budni," was the only retail chain to sell fritz exclusively and to have delisted Coca-Cola. To our great pleasure, they explicitly referred to our reusability strategy in justifying that decision. At the time, their more than 150 locations were to sell only reusable bottles. Only when Budni joined a purchasing syndicate that included the Edeka chain of supermarkets did they reintroduce Coca-Cola and single-use recyclable bottles.

We were also very pleased to receive a call from the caterer responsible for Airbus, inviting us to install fritz vending machines in their Hamburg-Finkenwerder aeronautics facility. At least the ace designers there have access to a sustainable "fuel," which will hopefully inspire them to develop more climate-friendly airplane engines.

We initially expanded our palette in our very first year of business. We've been offering an apple juice spritzer (now called *fritz-spritz*), an apple-cherry spritzer (now *apple-cherry-elderberry soda*), a melon seltzer (now *melon soda*), and a lemon soda since 2004. Our orange soda joined the family in 2008, and the family went back to nature in the early 2010s. It bothered us that none of the colorful soft drinks on the market contained real

ingredients. Sugar was usually the most natural thing listed on the label. Until 2011 it would have been hard to say whether a melon had ever been in the same room as our melon soda, and it certainly never made it into the bottle. Everything was based on artificial flavorings.

At some point it became clear to us that if we wanted to be better and more sustainable, we were going to need authentic, natural recipes. Therefore, we banished artificial flavorings and colorings from our all our products and started our first forays into the world of organics. Our years of experience eased the process greatly.

But many fans found the transition to be challenging. Our original melon soda tasted just like a fresh, juicy melon, and the green color really popped in the sunlight. That variety was extremely popular and successful. The downside was that the flavors and colors were so fresh and bright because they were artificial, so it was a popular variety without any real, authentic flavors. That's why we reformulated it to use real melon juice concentrate and natural flavorings — including real melon flavor — and the color became a yellowish green derived from Mexican safflower.

We used a similar approach to the fritz-kola coffee seltzer: out with artificial junk; in with natural ingredients. As soon as the first bottles were shipped, outcry spread through the ranks of our fans: "We want the artificial swill back!" So for a limited time, we reintroduced the melon soda and the coffee seltzer with modified labels under a sub-brand called *fritzi's melon art "pretty art-ificial."* That allowed hardcore fans of the old recipes to build up some reserve supplies.

I noticed at the time to what extent my sense of taste had become accustomed to artificial flavors. Initially, I also thought that the natural soft drinks tasted a little less awesome. People still ask me from time to time about that "awesome artificial melon soda." But it was important for us to take that step toward a more natural approach.

Another entry in the "more authentic and natural" books is that we diverge from almost all our competitors when it comes to "harmonizing" flavors. Most producers resort to artificial flavorings, instead of natural ingredients like spices and fruit juice, to achieve the taste of their products. One reason is that they want to achieve consistent quality in their drinks and to free themselves from seasonal variations in the taste of fruit. We use flavorings and extracts derived directly from the fruits after which our beverages are named. Our fans value authenticity and keeping it real, and we owe it to them.

And it's just a fact that fritz-beverages won't always taste exactly the same. That's nature.

For me, initiating processes of change from time to time is part of an entrepreneur's job. In 2012 we mixed our kola and our orange soda for the first time into a blended kola beverage, and thanks to one of Lorenz's brilliant ideas, we called it *mischmasch*.

As early as 2006, we expanded our kola line with a slimmer sibling: fritz-kola sugar free (which we now call "fritz-kola without sugar"). That was a difficult decision, and we hesitated for quite a while. A kola that's popular for its effects and the buzz it produces needs both caffeine and sugar. But our fans, especially the guys and gals from the hospitality industry, kept bugging us and eventually wore us down, so we developed a new recipe.

In 2008 we took a bit of a risk with the decision to offer our drinks in even smaller bottles. Our 330 ml bottles were shutting us out of a certain segment of the hospitality business. The 330 ml beer bottles are perfect for kiosks, snack bars, and diners, but 200 ml bottles are the uncontested industry standard in bars and places that serve cocktails, where guests expect more ambience and better service. Several bar owners had long been hinting at us that they would list fritz-kola as soon as we started offering 200 ml bottles. Christian Himmler, a

Hamburg native who ran eight watering holes around Hans-Albers-Platz square in the St. Pauli district of Hamburg at the time, liked us and our product for that reason alone. And he liked the taste of fritz-kola too. But no matter how doggedly Lorenz tried, he wasn't willing to experiment with it in all of his locations because only 300 ml bottles were available. He wouldn't dare more than a test run in two bars, neither of which yielded much in the way of results because his guests wanted to see that a fresh bottle was being opened and used up for each cocktail. Smaller bottles are also more common for beverages drunk to accompany meals in the fine dining segment. And since many other non-alcoholic beverages are sold in 200 ml bottles, our beer bottle would have messed up the whole price structure because ours would have necessarily been more expensive than the other soft drinks. Event dining and themed restaurants need smaller bottles because they need a wider margin on the beverages. Beverage margins are *the* cornerstone of the bar and restaurant business.

We recognized that we desperately needed smaller fritz-kola bottles. Our brand had to be where people were enjoying special evenings, where they would associate a positive feeling with our fritz-kola. In contrast to the beer bottles, this time we wanted exclusive fritz bottles with a unique design and our unmistakable logo. In order to have such bottles and the requisite crates produced in sufficient quantities, we needed more capital than we would have been able to scrape together. We were talking about 160 pallets, each containing 56 crates of 24 bottles a piece — more than 200,000 bottles of just fritz-kola at one fell swoop. But we were launching the new 200 ml bottles for all our varieties simultaneously, which added up to over 2.2 million bottles.

To make this undertaking a success, we took out a loan for 500,000 euros from the Hamburger Sparkasse bank. It was a calculated risk because we already knew who was going to produce, fill, and deliver the bottles, and we were sure that the market launch was going to be successful. The signals we had been receiving from our customers and sales reps were absolutely clear. And we knew that we were going to be able to pay the loan off in full very quickly, which we did. But it still left us breathless when the ink was dry. For someone who had been a college student with 7,000 euros of startup capital only five years previously, a loan for half a million is a decent chunk of change.

Taking inspiration from the big Carlsberg bottles, which I quite liked, I designed the shape of our new 200 ml bottles myself with Lorenz's blessing. Designing, financing, and arranging the production of our own bottle was a massive job for our little team. We had little time for anything else over the course of weeks.

When Lorenz first presented the new bottle to Christian Himmler, he said, "This is the coolest bottle I've ever held." With that, we knew we had done everything right. But today I must admit that, even though our do-it-yourself approach was true to fritz, we could have achieved an even better result had we sought more outside expertise and considered further aspects. How does the bottle look in a refrigerator? Does the size harmonize with the color? When we were developing the successor model to our 200 ml bottle in the fall of 2019, we had people on staff with more experience in that sort of thing than we had. Our sales lead, Chris Gröne, for one, could lecture for hours on shelf impact, referring to the impact a bottle should have when seen in a fridge and how we could find that out. He brought us the necessary external expertise. The new appearance is closer to that of our 330 ml "beer" bottle because that's what made us famous, and people associate us with it. Moreover, our new bottle is a bit more angular because we, as fritz-kola, come across as a bit more jagged and masculine.

We achieved a nice little triumph in 2011. We had been closely monitoring the discussion in the European Union

(EU) about the approval of stevia as a sweetener to reduce the amount of sugar in foods, and we had been preparing for it to pass. We launched our stevia-kola in December 2011, very soon after the EU approval went through. We already had the recipe and the label design saved on our desktops in anticipation of that moment. Being first was very important to us. And we were. We didn't even really have to hurry very much. Not until more than a year later did the story circulate in the media that Coca-Cola was testing a cola sweetened with stevia in Argentina and was planning to introduce it in Europe at some point in the future. And the shade of green they used on the label bears an incredibly striking resemblance to ours.

We reacted with a facetious ad in which we congratulated Coca-Cola on their revolutionary invention and included a subtle reminder that we had launched ours a year earlier.

It was great fun and attracted plenty of attention. Anyone with a sense of humor was with us. But to be honest, our stevia kola, which we called "fritz-kola, less sugar," never sold too well. We pulled it in 2020. The buzz around stevia turned out to be mostly hype that dissipated as quickly as it had arisen. For another thing, beverages sweetened with stevia still contain some sugar, which deterred those who were looking for salvation from "evil" sugar. In the end, not enough customers were interested in kola with less sugar. It's either full sugar or none.

In 2014 we launched a new product line called "fritz-spritz." It includes three organic spritzers: one with rhubarb juice, one with grape juice, and one with apple juice, which we've renamed fritz-spritz. In response to popular demand, since 2014 we have also been bottling our beverages in 500 ml bottles with screw caps, which are easier to open without a bottle opener and to reclose on the go. The shape of the 500 ml bottle doesn't match our other fritz-kola bottles at all, but it's the only standard-sized bottle with a screw cap that our customers can return for deposit anywhere.

a pineapple soft drink from 1952 joins fritz

The last Anjola pineapple soda was sold in 2010 at Bei Schorsch, a legendary snack bar in Hamburg. Johannes Gleske, a businessman, developed it in the Altona district of Hamburg in 1952, just in time to meet the demand in post-war Germany for all things exotic. But times had changed, and 2008 was the last year that any was produced in East Frisia, a region in the northwest of

Germany. As soon as Artur Hunger, the snack bar's owner, heard "Nope, we ain't gonna be makin' that no more," he stockpiled the last bright green crates full of the unique, pineapple-shaped glass bottles. Since the plant in East Frisia didn't want to deliver "all the way" to nearby Hamburg, Hunger rented a pickup truck, drove to Grossefehn and returned with 190 bright green crates of 20 bottles apiece back to Pferdemarkt Boulevard.

But the carbonated fruit-juice beverage was beloved well beyond Hamburg's city limits. Fans loved it because it wasn't produced by a huge conglomerate, it wasn't available just anywhere, it had a distinctive flavor, and the little round bottles made very cute vases. Something tasteful remained even after the bottle was empty.

We had encountered the Anjola brand back in the 1990s, when it was served in nightspots, and we were up for something new. So in 2011 we started asking the family that owned it about whether they'd be interested in an acquisition, which then occurred in 2013. It might have seemed like positioning the new brand was part of some preconceived grand plan of ours. But in fact, success had made us so confident and spoiled that we figured we could just sort out the details at our leisure after completing the takeover. After all, we had been in business for all of ten years by that point, we had a network of sales

TRINKT *Anjola*

reps, we knew how to make soft drinks, and we had no doubt in our abilities. We wanted to get everything exactly right. But what does that mean exactly? What followed was a lesson in what, I have since concluded, one should *not* do. We at fritz-kola had unconsciously been defining our purpose, our *raison d'être*, our calling. fritz-kola had always meant waking up, independence, doing our thing, not conforming, and standing up to the world leader. But how did Anjola reflect this purpose, this internal motivation? We two founders sat there, spoiled by success and flush with cash, but with completely different interpretations of the previous years, and we couldn't find any common ground for Anjola. So we fiddled with it until 2015, when we finally relaunched Anjola with a modern version of the bottle and five new recipes: a homemade kola and four sodas, including ginger, mate (a tea made with yerba mate), orange, and pineapple. A good seven years had passed since it had stopped being produced, and in the fast-paced beverage business, it had largely dropped out of popular consciousness.

We got started with the new Anjola, and we gave it everything we had to give at the time: all organic and/or fair-trade ingredients, a kola variety that was actually handmade (the production was brutally labor-intensive and cost a fortune), fruity varieties that were sweet and tasty, the mate was uniformly beloved throughout the office, and the ginger soda was a symphony of zing. We had invested a fortune in the bottling, the crates, and the bottles, and we were ready to go.

Unfortunately, it was already becoming apparent that Lorenz and I were no longer entirely on the same page as co-owners and hands-on entrepreneurs. It was becoming increasingly difficult for us to make good decisions together. So Anjola started with its own branding and sales team, which meant — depending on your point of view — that it either had to get by without the strength of our fritz-kola or that a firewall had to be erected to prevent the fritz-kola team from becoming distracted.

The episode ended with us going our separate ways as co-owners at the end of 2016, and soon thereafter we had to pull all varieties except the original Anjola pineapple. That decision was very painful for me, but after seriously adjusting our ownership structure and composition, we had to focus only on what was most important, which included discontinuing the less-popular varieties. Our first attempt to revive Anjola, the venerated brand, was a resounding failure.

We have since been able to establish Anjola as another brand in our portfolio after giving it another try in 2020. But it remains a lesson to me that we did everything right with only 7,000 euros in 2003 and made so many mistakes ten years later with a large multiple of that sum.

We were ignoring the fact that our passion for the brand had more to do with sentimentality and local pride. We weren't asking ourselves why Anjola was only available at one location in Hamburg and whether we could really manage to reverse the brand's downward spiral over the course of years. We naïvely projected

Anjola's success based on what we had achieved with fritz-kola, and we simply got ahead of ourselves. Reviving Anjola would probably have been very difficult even without the deepening rift between us. Only since we started devoting thorough planning and attention to the brand has the revival worked. Now Anjola gives us all a lot of joy.

tweaking the relaunch

Our corporation got a new name around the same time as the Anjola relaunch from fritz-kola LLC to *fritzkulturgüter* (fritz cultural goods) LLC. As for why we did this, there is a clever answer and an honest one. The clever answer is that we're the transmitters of valuable cultural goods, like really good kola and soft drinks, so the new name suits us better. The honest answer is that, prior to launching Anjola, we got the idea stuck in our heads that we would be making it difficult for the new brand to make its own impact if the shipments were coming from an entity called fritz-kola. So we renamed our LLC in September 2014. It was completely unnecessary in retrospect, although it did cost plenty of time and money. Customers buying directly from us would already know that Anjola and fritz-kola were under one roof — they were ordering it from us. And the consumers couldn't care less who was distributing whatever soft drink they had in their hands.

We had become victims of our perspective, seeing things only from the inside, which is common in enterprises and institutions. We sit in our bubbles and think thoughts shared by no one on the outside, or conversely become blind to things that are obvious to everyone on the outside. That's why, before investing in expensive innovation or relabeling projects, it's important to conduct sufficient "Average-Joe tests," which entail asking people unfamiliar with the arcane and sometimes peculiar corporate culture simply to react to what they see.

Our selection has been expanding rapidly since 2016, as it has for other, often-new entrants into the soft drink market. Consumers can choose from among constantly changing product palettes, even as retailers groan under the burden of such variety. fritz-mate — made with mate tea — complemented our selection in 2016, and organic fritz-kola with organically grown ingredients joined in 2018 as a further innovation. And we've always kept learning. When we began, I didn't realize how much the senses of sight and touch affect taste. That's why we now put so much stock in appealing, well-designed bottles. And you can taste what's printed on the label. Red berries are ripe and sweet; green ones are more tart and refreshing. That's how we all tick, because it's what we've learned as consumers. Psychology is a big part of the food industry.

Our internal structures are constantly becoming more specialized and professional. What for years could be improvised or managed on the fly now requires regular meetings and discussions with agendas and minutes, and must be implemented by those responsible according to the previously agreed plan. It wouldn't work otherwise with so many fritzes.

The trick is to remain agile despite the specialization and structure. It is practically a law of nature that enterprises become more bureaucratic as they grow. Many large companies are far too preoccupied with just managing themselves instead of being productive and creative, but it's not inevitable. For example, you have to remind yourself what it's really all about. What's important, and what do we have to do? What's unimportant and expendable? It can be a difficult exercise for people with lots of creative ideas — like me, for example. It can help to have someone on the team take a soberer look at the big picture. In my case, that would be my codirector Winfried Rübsam, who came to us with plenty of outside experience in 2017. Thanks to him, our haphazard heap has become a well-structured enterprise.

There isn't much you can do against the law of nature stating that the 300th employee will make a relatively smaller impact on the company's performance than the third new hire at the beginning. Conversely, though, equating small with better is too simplistic. I'm sometimes asked about that in reference to the many small producers offering coffee from artisanal roasteries or to neighborhood craft breweries. Of course, small *can* be better because it allows for more flexibility and individual treatment, but that's not automatically the case. Size has its benefits too, like being able to penetrate the market and having a say in the terms of deals. Size also means earning enough money to be independent and not having to cave too quickly in tough negotiations, like when a customer is threatening to delist a product in order to compel a discount. Staying strong and saying no could have fatal consequences for a smaller business. Size lets us do our thing and thrive in the market. Take, for instance, our cherished project of really encouraging reusable glass bottles. From what the glassworks that make our bottles tell us, almost nobody brings as many "ale longnecks" — clear, reusable 330 ml beer bottles — into circulation as we do. Our brand is so attractive to customers and retailers that they actively seek us out. When a chain of supermarkets in the Netherlands was prepared to list us, but only on the condition that we delivered in single-use recyclable glass bottles, we turned them down, remarking that we only offer reusables in the Netherlands. Another chain has since listed us — with reusable glass bottles. We could afford to wait until someone in that market was ready to make an attractive offer to environmentally conscious consumers.

And generally speaking, our size also helps us to take a stand on socially relevant issues and to have our voice be heard. We can serve as a point of reference in turbulent times, perhaps by taking a strong stance against xeno-phobia and making it clear that such attitudes are not okay.

But of course, I often ponder what the ideal size and structure of a company is. It is desirable that people who work together know and feel connected to each other. And it won't do for employees to lose regular and uninhibited contact with management because the latter might lose touch with the team. Such encounters motivate both sides and reinforce the sense in everyone that they're pursuing a common goal. It would be easy to follow a seemingly simple rule, like splitting up business units whenever they amass more than, say, a hundred members. But it's not that easy, because doing so would compromise the core idea and culture behind the company. The sense of camaraderie that emerges from this central identity is crucial for the staff and the success of the enterprise.

But to be perfectly honest, if Lorenz and I could have entered a time machine in 2003 to visit the fritz-kola of today, we probably would have said that we never wanted things to get so complicated. Our current coordination procedures take considerably longer than they did ten years ago, but the result is work of better quality and less overtime.

And I always return to the question of the right form for the company. Considering a company's size and structure are part of the internal deliberations regarding the proper mode of organization and how to meet current challenges. Such fundamental discussions revitalize us and keep us awake. If they are conducted constantly, such dialogue can get irritating, but big questions should never be taboo either.

As Lorenz was leaving the company, I looked into the prospect of going public in the course of searching for new investors. But I came to the conclusion that taking that step along with the concomitant dependence on

anonymous shareholders would clash with our culture and with the image we have of ourselves. It's more interesting to remain a real indie brand and to walk to the beat of our own drum. It allows us to dare to balance between the fritzes who've stayed with us, growing together, for a long time and new fritzes who push us forward with new experiences and ideas. We have to stay profitable even without a listing on the stock exchange, of course, but we don't have to scramble from one quarterly report to the next. We can take the long view instead.

Insourcing our bookkeeping was one of the first steps toward greater professionalization, and Rabea Haase assumed these duties in 2010. When we hired her, we had already reached the conclusion that this hire was more about finding someone with fritz-compatible DNA than about technical proficiency and qualifications. And she most certainly fit the bill: she was a trained book-keeper and had done articling as an accountancy clerk. It was an advantage that Rabea didn't belong to fritz's (hard partying) target market. A bookkeeper should have a sober disposition. That she also turned out to be such a fine person was an added bonus.

Our job posting indicated that we were looking for a full-time employee. But Rabea wanted to keep pursuing her business degree while working for us, and she was ready to give the degree priority if push came to shove. I'm of the opinion that an employer should be flexible in such situations. If you're sure you've found the ideal candidate, showing generosity toward their personal preferences is the right approach. You'll be repaid in commitment and loyalty.

When Rabea Haase joined our ranks in Liebig St., the small staff were spread out over the open-plan office and the warehouse, as she remembers:

Lorenz and Mirco each had an office at the end of the open-plan space separated from the rest with glass, and Lorenz used blinds to make his window opaque. Nonetheless, the whole physical layout suggested openness and transparency. But not for me. One side of my "office" was Lorenz's window, which was covered in blinds. In front of me, there was the back side of a filing cabinet, and there was a window to my right, so there was only one way to access my desk. The walkway was nearly blocked by another cabinet and two potted palm trees, which I had to squeeze through every morning to reach my workspace. The point of this peculiar interior design was to ensure that nobody could cast an unauthorized glance at the documents on my desk or at my monitor. It was also driven home to all my coworkers that nobody was to approach my desk when I wasn't there. No document could be left lying

around, even for just a short absence because Mirco and Lorenz very highly valued discretion in regard to our numbers. Revenue, profit, terms, and later even the actual number of employees were all secret. No outsider was to be able to infer our business relationships or push for better terms on the basis of our numbers.

Other than that, the atmosphere was very relaxed. Any hierarchies that existed were very flat. When the bosses were in the office and not (as usual) on the road building and maintaining business relationships, anyone could approach anyone else without much fuss. Work hours also operated on a kind of honor system. Specifically, overtime was considered "voluntary commitment," but absences during normal working hours were okay so long as they had been cleared with Mirco or Lorenz.

There was a team breakfast every Friday, which also served as an informal staff meeting. The bosses and the sales reps would come, and we'd discuss all the relevant issues and latest news. Team activities were also common in the early years of fritz. To celebrate winning the 2010 Founder Prize, we produced a "golden kola." All available staff sat in the office and glued, by hand, golden labels onto the 200 ml kola bottles. Applying stamps to the Christmas cards and newsletters were other activities we often did together. I dearly miss that kind of atmosphere.

I could watch how rapidly the enterprise was growing in the subsequent years from my own department. A temp eventually came to assist me, and she was so good that she was hired outright and works at fritz to this day. When I took parental leave in 2018, I was in charge of six people in the finance and accounting department.

Let me add something here: we never had much appetite for transparency when it came to the numbers. Rabea listed a few reasons. I now consider internal transparency about business-related figures to be absolutely vital. From experience, I know that it doesn't pay to advertise the business's numbers lest they fall into the hands of beverage-industry competitors and others who like to use scare tactics. Moreover, it's a pity when money dominates discussion about business and, instead of looking at the product, what a company actually makes, what it does, talk devolves into a mere comparison of performance indicators. We'd rather use the attention to talk about our kola and soft drinks than about our figures.

In regards to overtime, we certainly did benefit from our startup culture in the beginning, with everyone working a little more and with more freedom to experiment than they'd normally have. But today we keep an eye on working hours. Specifically, we cultivate

an atmosphere in which it's okay for anyone to say that they're feeling overworked. Generally speaking, business email and phone calls are taboo in the evenings and on weekends.

It is now apparent that, if properly implemented, using the honor system for work hours and mixing hours spent working in the office and at home brings some real benefits, because everyone concerned can combine work, family, and leisure time more flexibly. We have already learned a lot from the continuing experience with everyone working exclusively from home during the COVID pandemic. On the one hand, the relevance of office-based work culture has dropped. On the other, there's more communication about what work can realistically be completed in what timeframe, which tasks have priority, and which can wait. How can we protect ourselves from burning out when work no longer has any limits, and we can work 24/7 because the distinction between home and office has collapsed? How do teams collaborate when they only see each other through a screen? As it stands today, I suspect that the honor system and flexibility in terms of being present in the office are here to stay post-COVID.

Many have come to appreciate the ability to find a better, more flexible balance between private appointments, family life, and work. At the same time, everyone involved has to tolerate a degree of uncertainty with regard to the actual number of hours worked, and they have to make sure that neither employee nor employer takes advantage of the other.

From my perspective, there is little danger of people being compelled to work too much or doing so for fear of losing their job as long as the shortage of qualified labor persists. There are enough companies looking to hire and eager to find candidates for their open positions. It'll be interesting to see what happens when the labor market shifts and the supply of labor outstrips demand.

Without a doubt, many who work for early-stage startups work longer hours and less predictably than it states in their contracts, and maybe even for very modest pay. Those who are up for it foremost gain the chance to grow, in addition to opportunities for advancement and a broad range of tasks. As long as hierarchies remain flat, responsibility and knowledge are free for the taking, which could pay off — literally — at the next job, perhaps for a conglomerate. We've seen this ourselves. Young people come to work for fritz-kola for a few years, work a lot, learn a lot, and then move on. The founders and staff of startups, men and women alike, tend to be pretty young and rarely have families of their own. They usually

identify very deeply with the company and its products, and they'd feel more constrained than liberated by a regimented nine-to-five mentality.

Setting up our purchasing management was a typical process in the course of our growth. At a trade show in 2014 or 2015, Juan Gravalos, our sales manager for Germany, Austria, and Switzerland, was talking with the oft-mentioned Peter, who had since become a key account manager at his company. They were discussing the recurring bottlenecks and organizational gaps that were regularly slowing production. Peter said, "What you need is supply management, somebody from the beverage industry to help you get your inventory throughput working properly." To which Juan replied, "Why don't you do it?!" And that's how Peter came to fritz, where he managed our purchasing department from 2015 to 2019. That team is responsible for making sure that the right things of the right quality get to the right place at the right time. They're in charge of raw ingredients, crates, labels, and bottling capacity. They're also responsible for quality control, which had previously been the responsibility of everyone and no one. Managing the supply chain for frictionless production has always been and remains a huge challenge because of our dynamic growth. We were constantly hiring more caffex (sales fritzes), and the bottling plants sometimes had trouble keeping up. That was less a problem of money than of resources not growing fast enough. It was like Tesla's current problem on a smaller scale: more people want to buy the product than can be supplied in the short term. Of course, that kind of situation is more pleasant than the opposite, but it's still stressful.

the cycle of returnable bottles

pools and the deposit loophole

Whereas many countries have deposit schemes to make sure bottles and cans are recycled, Germany has a tiered system that includes recyclable bottles without deposit (for example, for wine and some juices), recyclable glass, plastic, and aluminum containers that bear a deposit and are melted down (for example, beverage cans, some soft drinks, and discount beers), and reusable bottles that are washed, refilled, and sent back out into circulation with a hefty deposit (for example, for beer, mineral water, and premium soft drinks). At fritz-kola, we use reusable and refillable bottles whenever possible.

Obviously, empty bottles shouldn't have to be shipped very far. Therefore, it makes sense to have uniform bottles for different beverages, which can be on the move between various producers and customers in open pools. These pools aren't actively managed, and everyone can do as they please. This is common practice among most breweries and for us too. The alternative is for various beverage producers to manage a closed pool of uniform bottles together, such as the *Genossenschaft Deutscher Brunnen* (German Spring Water Cooperative) with their spring-water bottles, and the fruit juice-industry association with their one-liter fruit juice bottles

("AF" bottles in Austria). It makes no difference whether a bottle goes back to where it was last filled or to another plant. That becomes apparent when returning bottles to the beverage store: they aren't usually sorted by brand in each crate, but rather Bionade and fritz bottles can be combined because they're both standard, clear 330 ml bottles. Once the labels have been washed off before refilling, the bottles are identical. Upon filling, the bottles are relabeled according to brand and go back into circulation among customers and consumers.

Custom bottles, which are used by a single beverage producer and must always be returned to the bottling plant from which they originated, work differently. These bottles offer the advantage of greater customization in that a brand can express itself more visually. The disadvantage is in the greater shipping distances required because they must be returned to a particular bottling plant and cannot be washed and refilled by another producer. This is the case, for example, with the 200 ml fritz-kola bottles for our customers in the hospitality industry. We only use these because "fritz-kola" is embossed in the glass. We avoid the longer distances that the custom bottles typically require with our network of local bottling plants. This gives all our reusable glass bottles a short trip out to quench a customer's thirst and then back to us.

Anyone entering the beverage market with only a single bottling location is thus well advised to join a bottle pool or a deposit pool, including bottles and crates, to be able to deliver their beverages with the shortest, most environmentally friendly route possible.

When Germany introduced a mandatory deposit on recyclable beverage packages in 2003, a new, unintended source of revenue emerged for beverage producers called "the deposit loophole." This refers to the profit that accrues to beverage producers when they take customers' deposits for all the bottles sold, but not all bottles are returned. The point of sale turns a profit for every carded bottle that isn't returned.

The deposit loophole applies to both reusable glass pool bottles, as described above, as well as to single-use recyclable bottles, which are generally made of plastic. The difference is that the deposit on reusable glass bottles has traditionally been calculated with reference to the production cost of the bottles and tends to be a little lower, whereas the single-use, recyclable plastic bottles have a legally standard deposit of 0.25 euro per bottle, which is far higher than the production cost. Therefore, the greater difference between deposit and production cost on the single-use recyclables means that the deposit loophole is much more lucrative in their case.

Cynics have been known to claim that discounters make more profit on the deposit loophole on their house-brand water and soft drinks, which are sold in single-use recyclable plastic bottles that carry a 0.25-euro deposit, than on the beverages contained inside. This might be an exaggeration, but if so, it is a small one.

misadventures, crises, and mistakes

There is no business without the occasional misstep and odd calamity. Any corporate history would be incomplete and implausible without them. If I were to claim that everything always ran smoothly and there were never any serious problems, it would imply that our company employed robots, not people.

I doubt there's any entrepreneur who would seriously deny ever having made a mistake or survived a crisis. Choosing to be an entrepreneur coincides with a higher appetite for risk and the drive to try stuff out — the danger of making mistakes, of failing, and of tumbling into crises is already priced in. Blunders and crises are part of the job description. At a meeting of entrepreneurs, one participant told me that "only rough seas make true entrepreneurs." There's probably some truth to that.

Slipups are the occurrences you can laugh about later and that make for great anecdotes to tell at the conference reception. But they cause white knuckles and plenty of cold sweat while they're happening. Take, for example, the time when a truck transporting our empties had an accident on the autobahn in 2008. Fortunately, nobody was hurt except for the thousands of bottles smashed on the asphalt. Call it a reverse-deposit-loophole, if you will.

Speaking of the autobahn, I'm reminded of some of our trips back in 2003, our first year. At some point I had borrowed a trailer from my father that was much larger than my old VW van, which was towing it. Fully loaded with empties on the way to the brewery, and then even more on the way back with freshly filled kola crates, the trailer was far too heavy for my van. We endured crossing the Weser Uplands a few times in second gear and then later driving through the depths of the Elbe Tunnel in Hamburg at less than 20 miles per hour. Other drivers were cursing loudly behind me. Sorry folks. After that trip, we always rented a 7.5-ton truck to pick up the crates.

The year 2008 was our year. We were very proud to finally have our own fritz-kola bottle. After a long process of design, technical adjustments in the bottling process, and taking out our first loan, the time had come. Our new, fancy 200 ml super-bar-café-restaurant bottles of fritz soft drinks filled a huge warehouse. We could have easily financed and produced a year's output. We roughly guesstimated how much we could realistically expect to sell. How many of our customers in the bar and restaurant business would switch to these exclusive new bottles we were producing just for them. How many new customers could we expect to gain?

The grand launching ceremony took place at the Internorga, the biggest German hospitality trade show held in Hamburg. My college girlfriend Lydia, who had very conscientiously proofread my final thesis paper, came to meet us at the stand. Casually sipping at some fritz-kola, she was examining our bottles with a curious expression. "Hey Mirco," she called me over. "Why does sugar appear right after water on the list of ingredients for 'sugar-free fritz-kola'?"

I almost collapsed in fright. I grabbed the bottle and read it for myself. Sugar was actually listed as an ingredient on the label of the new 200 ml bottles of sugar-free fritz-kola. I opened a bottle and tasted the kola. The recipe had definitely used artificial sweetener, not sugar. So the devil in the details had only found his way into the printing of the labels, not the bottling of the

product. Thank heavens. But how could that have happened? The labels had gone back and forth endlessly between us and the graphic designers before printing. We had checked everything countless times, but this error slipped by regardless. Mistakes like this are the last thing anyone needs.

But 2008 went very well for us otherwise. Many people wanted to have our kola, and we were newly listed in a series of supermarkets. To keep these supermarkets fully stocked, for each crate of fritz-kola newly listed in a supermarket, we needed to keep roughly one more crate in the intermediating beverage distributor, another in our warehouse, and another in production. That meant that, for each crate that was available for sale on a supermarket shelf, we had to finance and purchase the materials and service for an additional three reusable crates, and 3 x 24 empty reusable bottles. Ouch. But having just taken out one loan, we didn't want to have to go trudging back to our local bank to borrow even more money.

We came up with the idea of temporarily packing our 330 ml reusable bottles in cardboard boxes and delivering these to the supermarkets, which generally sold the bottles in smaller quantities anyway. There was a machine to pack cardboard boxes sitting around at the bottling plant, and our sales volumes to supermarkets were miniscule at the time. The empty bottles returned for deposit would land in other producers' crates for a while, which would buy us time to finance and purchase more reusable crates of our own. We sold more single bottles and six packs than full crates back then anyway. For all the individual customers cared, a cardboard box was just as good as a six pack.

But shipping the cardboard boxes was a complete nightmare. The beverage distributors refused to accept the boxes, insisting that our goods be delivered in crates instead. Delivering to all the new supermarkets ourselves, as we had done a few years prior, was no longer on an option. We had gotten too big. Groan. We were stuck between being too small to finance new undertakings and too big to deliver ourselves.

There was nothing to be done except marshaling all of our numbers together and going back to the bank to ask for money. At the time, I had the impression that it had served us well to have all the numbers tabulated by an accountant using proper accrual accounting rather than the simpler cash-basis accounting method. It was more complicated and expensive, but we could always provide good, robust figures when meeting with the bank. That's how we finagled another load of reusable crates. While we did lose a few weeks (and some revenue), we

received new crates delivered to our door. It was time to summon all fritz's lads and lassies from the offices and sales to the Warehouse Olympics, where over the course of days we moved the bottles into crates from cardboard boxes, which we then folded. We kept those boxes for years, using them to send promotional items, samples, and so on. At least they weren't a total waste.

I described a few other serious crises above in the section on wannabes. Two of those instances turned out to be double crises in which a partner unexpectedly transformed into a competitor, costing us an important distributor too. We suddenly found ourselves with yet another product to compete with and fewer distribution channels to move our own. That sort of thing hits hard every time.

We also had to react swiftly and decisively when we discovered that one of our freelance sales reps was offering two crates of fritz-kola to a Premium Cola customer for the price he had been paying for each crate of Premium Cola. Muscling out the competition with such tactics was counter to our philosophy. We then officially and strictly forbade practices like that for everyone. Nevertheless, it left a bad taste in the mouths of many in the industry, and it damaged fritz-kola's reputation.

Shitstorms on social media are a relatively new form of crisis. Thanks to the internet's ability to spread content virally and to fire people up, valid criticism as well as exaggerated or completely fabricated accusations can build into a tidal wave against which reacting calmly and rationally becomes virtually impossible. I can remember two shitstorms that touched on fritz-kola's social stances. The first revolved around "Frei.Wild," a Deutschrock band from South Tyrol. The band attracts criticism for their

nationalist, chauvinist lyrics, among other things. At the same time, they're so popular that their albums are charting in Germany in the 2020s, and their concerts fill arenas. The band is very divisive, and they know how to make good use of the attention they attract. Nobody at fritz knew the band or their genre of music. After all, South Tyrol is 12 hours from Hamburg by car, but don't forget that there's no such thing as bad publicity. By the end of the episode, all of Hamburg had heard of this Austrian-Italian band.

It went something like this: Christian Himmler (aka "Himmy"), mentioned earlier, ran two independent bars, one in front of the other, at Hans-Albers-Platz square, near the Reeperbahn Boulevard in the St. Pauli district. In front, facing the square, was the *fritz-bar*, which is not part of our company. Of course, we were prominently placed in the bar, but we didn't receive a cut of the revenues, nor did we have any influence on their bookings. In the back, connected by a corridor, was the *Platzhirsch* — a location that could be booked for concerts and other events, like album launch parties. The only thing they had in common was the corridor that connected the one room to the other and the landlord.

We had no idea that the band had contacted Himmy in 2015 about renting the *Platzhirsch* for a meet-and-greet concert for their most devoted fans. Why should he tell us who's renting a room of his — one that had nothing to do with the *fritz-bar* and even less to do with fritz-kola? Himmy knew of the controversy surrounding the band, and he didn't personally find them fascist in spite of their dabbling with national-chauvinist elements. But to be on the safe side, he gave a Frei.Wild CD to a few of his people, including several immigrants, and asked them their opinions. Do you guys consider this an extremist band? No, they said, it's just garden-variety Deutschrock. It's not everyone's cup of kola, but it's a free country. Himmy went ahead and contractually booked the band.

And then Facebook blew up. One post called for people to "Chase Frei.Wild out of our neighborhood — no platform for nationalists in St. Pauli" and asked what we thought of the fact that Frei.Wild would be performing in the "fritz-bar/Platzhirsch." The dam was breaking. Through no fault of our own, we were being dragged into the middle of the controversy. Critical comments started to clog our Facebook page. To make matters worse, Himmy was on vacation in the United States as things started to boil over. I finally reached him and told him that fritz-kola was being dragged through the mud. Here's how Himmy describes his position:

I've never been a fan of the idea that anyone — radical

right or left — dares to decide who gets to hear what, say what, perform where, and go so far as to enforce their view with violence. It disgusts me when anyone who diverges a millimeter from a certain point of view gets branded a Nazi.

When Mirco called me in the United States, and we were agreed that trying to clarify the situation with statements was pointless, I contacted my lawyer with instructions to cancel the contract with Frei.Wild's management, against my own judgment and at a cost of about 10,000 euros. My principal motivation at the time was to help fritz-kola out of a tight spot because we're friends, because I like the brand, and because I'm grateful for what they've done in and for Hamburg. The concert then took place somewhere down in the harbor, without any incident.

This episode was so threatening to us for the same reason that all smear campaigns are threatening: something is bound to stick. Our sales reps had to be prepared for a vague sense of "fritz-kola supports a right-wing band" among our customers. The original poster didn't have to take any responsibility for the inaccurate information. The whole affair was really f---ed up because it damaged our reputation right in the heart of our top sales region. If the people who stood and stand by us had turned their backs on fritz, it would have been really hard for us.

A year and a half later, we witnessed for a second time how quickly outrage can take on a life of its own and become a force of habit. In February 2017, a woman named Melanie D., whom we had never heard of, posted a photo on Instagram showing her sipping from a fritz-kola bottle with her eyes closed. The caption: "fritz it up nicely." Our social media team replied in a friendly manner to the post, just like lots-n-lots of others that reach us each day. We posted, " … then keep on fritzing. We wish you lots-n-lots of refreshment." However, we didn't know at the time that Melanie D. was a rising star in right-wing extremist circles around Düsseldorf. Having been previously convicted of hate speech, she was a co-organizer of *Dügida*, the local Düsseldorf branch of the right-wing *Pegida* movement. Her post and our light-hearted reply touched a sore sport: as a local product, fritz-kola is not just a favorite among lefties and tree huggers, but among right-wing sympathizers as well, who see us primarily as a *German* alternative to Coca-Cola and want to instrumentalize us for their German chauvinism and xenophobic nationalism.

We then apologized for our error in a Facebook post and retracted our wishes for their refreshment in any form.

'sup dear fritz friends,

do you know melanie d.? we've known of her since this morning, thanks to you.

we don't have any contact with melanie d., nor are we flirting with her, nor with the ideology she stands for, nor with the right wing as a whole, for which we cannot muster even the least sympathy or understanding.

in accordance with our fundamentally courteous manner, we wished her "lots-n-lots of refreshment" yesterday without adequately checking into her background, her symbols, and her person. it backfired royally.

we receive several posts on instagram, facebook, and twitter each day, and we try to give each appropriate attention. we don't have any bots working for us, just people — people on a caffeine buzz who also make the occasional mistake. we made a mistake, and we're asking for your forgiveness.

we don't want to keep a blacklist of the right and wrong customers. the right-wing scene is not our thing, and we want to give them exactly the attention they deserve: none. anyone who knows us, knows our values, our sense of right, wrong, and responsibility also knows that we promote, support, and live tolerance and diversity, internally as well as from our customers and partners.

we thank you for your watchful eyes and tips, but please

consider that the increasing attention to this matter helps
one group most of all: ms. d. and her friends.
    on this note we wish #norefreshmentformelanie

p.s.: "fritz-kola" is spelled with a k, *melanie.*

At least in this instance there was a real basis for the
protest many users expressed on our pages, even if it was
due to a case of carelessness on our part. Remembering
that so many people were prepared to interpret such an
oversight as a political, pro-right-wing statement, I can
only shake my head even today. The social media team
at a company like ours cannot be expected to know all
the relevant names that would sound the alarm bells if
praise comes from the wrong corner. And social media
move so fast that thoroughly researching each post is
simply impractical. The upshot: shit happens, and
we'll have to live with it despite our best efforts and
intentions.

    We try to learn from these experiences, but it will
never be a fair fight. A company is obligated to tell the
truth, even if the other side lies through its teeth and facts
are forgotten in the heat of the moment. You have to react
quickly, respond to everything immediately, identify and
admit your mistakes, and correct inaccurate statements

right away. And you mustn't brush anything off, no matter how ridiculous it may seem.

One consequence of our growth is obvious: our underdog status is history, at least in northern Germany. In the words of Gerrit Lerch, one of our first customers, ""David and Goliath is over. fritz-kola has itself become a giant. Of course, something of the local flair has been lost." We might seem like a giant in the eyes of Schulterblatt St., the Schanze district, and the neighborhood around Hans-Albers-Platz square, but it's a different story five blocks away. But Gerrit's point is an important check on our collective self-perception and especially my own personal one. I still catch myself thinking "we're the plucky little guy." My staff, the many women and men who work hard for us every day, have to correct me sometimes and remind me how big and established we've become. A living, dynamic enterprise has grown out of that little student kola project.

Ivonne Anton, our head of human resources, has seen the inside of other companies and recently remarked in all seriousness that, "We're a professionally organized, medium-sized business with eight-digit revenues and nearly 300 employees." Perfectly normal, as far as it goes.

Another aspect of losing our underdog status is that the margin for error has shrunk. The public and our business partners alike are much less tolerant of cheeky little infractions and carelessness. The perception of fritz has changed, and people are right to expect that we act accordingly.

One benefit of our growth is that I have more time to get out there, out among the ones I care about, among our fritzes, our customers in bars, cafés, clubs, and out in the convenience stores, the independent merchants, and the beverage hustlers.

My role has changed dramatically, from the guy schlepping and hawking the crates to an entrepreneur with nearly 300 people: mothers, fathers, interns, bar experts, graphic designers … great people. When a company grows to fritz's size and so many livelihoods depend on it, then it's the owners' duty to make themselves expendable. It might sound odd at first, but when my cofounder left, we managed to reorganize the business and empower the people enough to keep it going even if I were run over by a bus tomorrow. For someone who founded the company and guided it down a long road, it's a weird situation at first to get over my own vanity and the idea that it won't work without me. Still, I can understand the many passionate entrepreneurs — usually men — who remain actively involved into their old age and keep going until the end.

it's great to be an entrepreneur

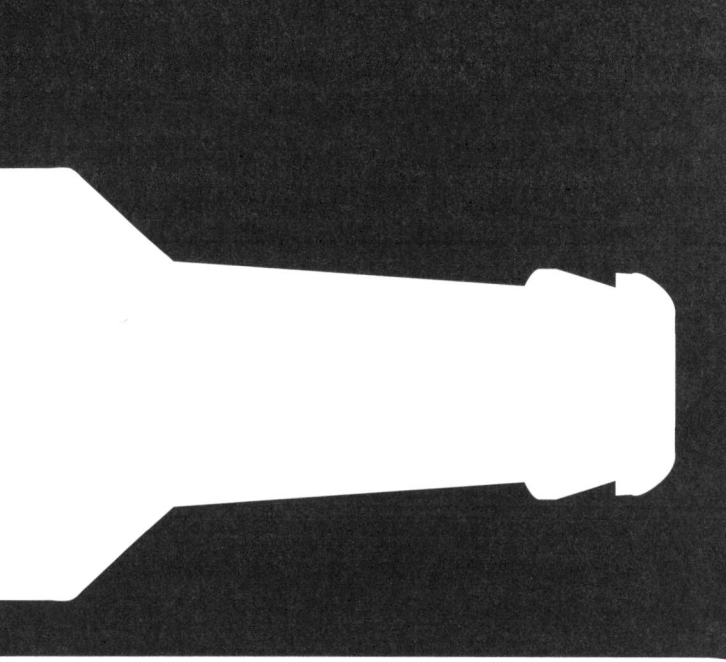

Among the qualities that, in my view, have proven to be the most important in my life as an entrepreneur are these that I learned as a Boy Scout: endurance and persistence.

mirco wolf wiegert

A little thought experiment: I'm now in my mid-forties. I have built, mostly together with Lorenz, a dynamic brand and a functioning enterprise and led it through tough times with our team. I could pack it in. I could sell my shares and be financially comfortable for the rest of my life. And then I could devote my time exclusively to things I like doing, without pressure and without stress. Where's the false premise? Simple: my work as an entrepreneur *is* what I like doing best.

I would describe my motivation to be an entrepreneur as follows. Imagine passing by the window of a candy store every morning. It's pure paradise. Among all the candies, chocolates, licorice ropes, the chocolate fountain, the soft-serve machine, the cotton candy, and the soft drinks of all descriptions is a sign that reads: "Take all you like!" You storm into the store and gorge yourself on the entire display until you're ready to burst. And the window is restocked the next morning, and you can go back and try everything again. That's what it's like for me every morning as an entrepreneur with all the opportunities and choices that are available to me. Sure, sometimes all the sweets give you a stomach ache, and sometimes you chip your tooth on a jawbreaker, but there are always so many cool things to try.

Another kind of entrepreneurial lifestyle can also be very interesting: the "serial entrepreneur," which entails founding one exciting business after another and guiding them to an exit, where they are adopted by professional hands. It's so much fun to be an entrepreneur and to do your own thing, even though it's lots-n-lots of work and responsibility. But being able to walk around in a hoodie, jeans, and sneakers all day is compensation enough for making fritz-kola.

Sometimes people ask me after a lecture whether earning lots of money was my motivation for becoming self-employed. I'm used to the question by now, even though it rather misses the point. My motivation comes from my passion for my thing, my project. That it can be lucrative in the best case is simply a welcome bonus.

In that respect, money is a means to an end. Beyond basic sustenance, it's useless until you do something with it. That's why I never sought to grow the company and its profits as quickly as possible only to sell it. For me, that would have been like building my dream house with my own hands, only then to sell it once the paint was dry instead of living in it.

I was never really as interested in possessing things (especially not something as abstract as monetary wealth) as in actually doing things. The root of the word

business is *busy*. And it seemed nonsensical to me to relinquish the opportunity at the precise moment that I gained the ability to effect change — in our market segment and in the wider society.

Entrepreneurs can find joy in shaping things, accepting or taking responsibility, the joy of independence, being as much the master of one's own fate as any of us can be, without having to ask permission from any bank, any investment fund, or any shareholders' meeting. At a certain point, we certainly could have grown faster and more aggressively, earning more money in less time. But at what price? We would have been sacrificing fritz-kola's independence, and we would have ended up doing things we didn't want to do.

We founders were always determined not to take on any outside investors or risky loans for speculative ventures or eggs that hadn't yet been laid. When we took out the loan to introduce the 200 ml bottles in 2008, we knew exactly what bills we would pay with the money and when we'd be able to pay it back. If it had been a gamble, leaving us to play the odds, we wouldn't have done it even if we had found someone to lend us the money.

People sometimes ask me whether it was really a good idea to opt for self-employment in Germany of all places. I can't even really answer the question for lack of a comparison. As founders and entrepreneurs, we've always been able to make good use of the advantages Germany offers. There's little corruption, and public safety is assured. And we still have outstanding industrial and satisfactory administrative infrastructures, especially in the urban centers and the surrounding areas. Open positions can generally be filled with well-educated candidates from several different cultures. Europe will hopefully close the tax loopholes for internet companies in the coming years so that all corporations do their part to maintain the existing infrastructure, not just the medium-sized businesses like us. It benefits us all. From our current vantage point in the middle of the COVID pandemic in 2021, it's interesting to watch how the several national economies pull themselves out of this serious crisis. Will the neoliberal ideology of "leave it up to the market" continue in the wealthier countries? Will it be possible to rebuild the infrastructure of both the government and the free market? Will we manage to heal the divisions in our society caused by resources, origins, and attitudes?

When we became founders in 2003, it wasn't yet very hip to be an entrepreneur. Second thoughts and envy among others were more widespread than they are now. Even today, there's an unspoken rule not to show one's

wealth and material success. It's considered uncouth. I'm no stranger to such understatement, but it's also interesting to watch the countervailing trend among the new generation of web entrepreneurs, the influencers and celebrities, who are much less reticent about showing off their success.

What happens when we give women and men who start their own business a social platform? Founding certainly has more cachet than it did 20 years ago. The encouraging and empowering startup atmosphere we know today was unheard of then. Considering the opportunities that are now available for virtual networking and reaching a wide audience, there should be far more founders than there are. I often receive invitations to attend founder conventions and seminars, and I beat the drum for the joy of entrepreneurship. We should be spreading the message in kindergartens, schools, and universities that pursuing one's own projects and being self-employed is perfectly normal. The need to determine the course of events is completely natural — perhaps not for everyone, but for many of us.

It is rewarding to talk with students and schoolkids who are dealing with the topic of entrepreneurship in their own projects and invite me to share my experience with them. Whenever I can fit it in, I attend two or three

such day-long appointments each year. While not all of the students want to be self-employed, of course, the penny drops for a few of them when they hear about how it can and does work. Those who are seriously interested come out feeling validated and motivated. I can really identify with that style of economic education.

When I talk to young people who are thinking about becoming entrepreneurs and they tell me about their ideas, I sometimes catch myself casting the same kinds of doubts that used to raise my hackles. Maybe it's due to my age, but it probably also has to do with my experience and how my standards have grown over the years of how thoroughly a business idea should be thought through. I've lost the carefree attitude I started with, of course, but I still try not to play the skeptical know-it-all in such

situations, drawing attention to open and difficult issues through targeted questions instead. I certainly want to help maintain their motivation and to focus more on the opportunities than on the risks. At the end of the day, I'm convinced that there's always room for new ideas, provided they're good ones. As an outsider, I want to see that someone has put a lot of thought into their project, that there's a clear plan, and that they've invested a lot of love into everything, in the details too. In such cases, the effort and the risk will often be richly rewarded. It's the same in the soft-drink business, which is incredibly dynamic and very innovative. Anyone trying to make their mark in it needs to find an open — and lucrative — niche and then conquer it, probably with a shoestring budget and lots-n-lots of work. My strategy has served me well, and perhaps it can help to inspire others: it's better to start small and achieve profitability immediately. That preserves your independence and lets you grow step by step. The greatest challenge is to build a brand and to build customers' trust in the brand. Reading an article recently, I underlined a statement from Roman Huber, the startup consultant, that remains true: "You're running a marathon, and there are ups and downs."

I help young founders where I can because a Europe-wide startup culture is very important to me and because

I want to share with others the fun and joy of starting a company.

what makes for a good entrepreneur?

Based on my experience, I believe many personality types are suited to entrepreneurship. Of course, one needs a certain mentality and a healthy hunger for independence to even dare founding a company. I've seen the following types: the fierce and the timid, the confident and the hesitant, the authoritarians and the softies, the charismatic and the vanilla. There are control freaks and easygoing types, risk junkies and strategists, the ruthless and the just, exploiters and caretakers, the penny-pinchers and the profligate, managers and patriarchs … So what follows in this chapter is about me, not about entrepreneurs in general.

I've already mentioned that I have the Boy Scouts to thank for my persistence. A typical situation among the Scouts might go something like this: you're out in the middle of the woods, taking a breather on the way to a predetermined destination, and it suddenly begins to rain buckets. Half of the provisions laid out for a trek of several days are wet and spoiled before you have time to react.

Most of the clothes are soaked along with the sleeping bags. Marching back to the start would take half a day, and it's two-and-a-half days to the destination. The Boy Scouts taught me how utterly unthinkable it is to choose the option of "turn around and give up." The course of action was always perfectly clear: we have to come up with a new plan to ration the supplies, and we'll dry the wet equipment by the fire, but we're going to reach our destination, crossing every river, traversing every valley, scaling every mountain. We will get there. I'm grateful that I was able to acquire an unshakeable will to persevere through tough situations.

Of course, I also learned how to assert myself in a group. Later, as a troop leader, I led and motivated a team. But adolescents operate on a different wavelength than adults in teams at work. Unfortunately, I wasn't able to directly apply much of what I learned to business.

Of course, I have changed in the nearly two decades since we founded the company. That's a logical corollary of my role and confidence in my own abilities. The more things work out for you, the more confident you become about new ventures. Still, I was never the kind of guy who walks through life with an inborn, unshakable sense of self-confidence.

I really am passionate about my product and my life as an entrepreneur. I had to learn, however, how to communicate my enthusiasm to others and get them on board with me. My work is my passion, so I have to be really careful not to see fritz-kola as my (only) home. Although it's work, I really love coming here, not the least because of the great people I get to work with.

Areas in which I still need to grow include delegation and letting go. I come from the school of "if you want a job done right …" and I didn't want to depend on anyone else. But as fritz-kola kept growing, I found that this attitude can also be limiting. I had to learn to ask others for advice. I used to hold myself to the standard of being able to do any job at least as well as the employee responsible for it. Our growth has taught me, though, that we need people in many positions who are light-years ahead of me in their respective areas. We're fortunate to have these people, and I'm happy to admit that our continued success depends on these fantastic individuals and their expertise.

How much leeway should I give my people? What can or must I do myself without strangling their initiative? That remains a sometimes-painful learning process, but it's necessary because over the years fritz-kola has outgrown the idea that the self-employed entrepreneur

can do everything himself. Introspection is an indispensable quality for an entrepreneur, and it can be productively channeled with the help of a good professional coach.

One typical aspect of my entrepreneurial personality is my instinct to cut costs down to the last cent. Some people might think, "Boy, he's tight fisted and drives a hard bargain," but I'm happy to hear that sort of thing. It's not about padding my bank account; it's about safeguarding the future of the fritz enterprise. My acute vigilance about money probably stems from my own experience of how hard money can be to come by. Besides that, I always have our fixed costs in mind, which we have to pay regardless of how well or poorly the business happens to be doing that month. Wages, benefits, rent, and so on don't go away. Thanks to my inborn vigilance and my interest in the topic, I know our balance sheet in considerable detail. And even though it's no longer part of my job, I could still negotiate individual deals, but perhaps not down to the fourth decimal place like I used to.

I still have great respect for my job and my responsibility as an entrepreneur. I don't take it for granted when things work out and go well. And I never forget what an immense responsibility I bear, not only directly for the fritzes, but also indirectly for the staff of the bottling plants, for example. We're often their largest customer, and they invest in expensive equipment because of us. Losing our business would be a major blow for many businesses. In a networked economy as we have, hundreds of people can depend directly and indirectly on a medium-sized business like ours.

Which brings us straight to the topic of leadership and leadership styles, because being an entrepreneur is synonymous with being a leader.

College unfortunately didn't prepare me very well for the leadership role I was going to assume. But leading people is a core competency required for founding and building a business. Inspiring others, ensuring that all members of a group and growing organization are working more or less toward the same goal, is part of the job from the very beginning, or at least no later than the initial growth phase. Sadly, leadership was not included in our famous loose-leaf business plan back in 2002 (but it should be part of every business plan). We weren't even thinking at the time about assembling a staff big enough to require a leadership strategy. And in those first years, we made a bunch of mistakes while trying to find the right leadership style.

Looking back, it occurs to me that my day-to-day work was sharply focused on making the kola into a successful

product to the neglect of leading the people we had hired. Many founders can probably relate. In those first years, everything has to run in parallel: product development, production, sales, dealing with the administrative stuff, client meetings, suppliers, the media, all those jobs "nobody else can do." And oh yeah, here are some more new faces in the office. Well, then I'll just do a performance evaluation too. Focusing on the core idea of the business just consumes everything. But a lot of the basic principles are quite simple; you just have to know them and take them to heart. What follows might sound completely banal, but in those first years I really screwed up majorly on these basic guidelines.

basics for entrepreneurs

- **Choose the right people.** Do I know what I want from them, and can they really deliver? Can I even find the right people? Especially in the early stages, it's tempting to hire whoever happens to be around. It's not always a bad policy. The motivation of new hires can compensate for a lot, but this practice is not strictly orthodox.
- **Don't discourage people.** Founders have to resist the temptation to do everything themselves and micro-manage others to the point where they can no longer see themselves in their own work, leaving them feeling like they're being denied their own competence and autonomy.
- **Know what you are trying to accomplish.** Why are doing this anyway — what's the point of it all? Meeting the challenge is impossible without certainty about the goals and the reasons for the effort.
- **Know your team.** What really drives people? What motivates them? One might be after a steady paycheck, another might want to be creative in all they do, and a third just wants to move up the ranks. Everyone has their own motives, but it's important to know them.
- **Clearly define goals and demand performance.** In

order to meet expectations, people need to know exactly what they are.

- **Know what's important to you as a founder.** What are your values, what are you willing to accept, and what's beyond the pale? Be transparent about where you stand. It will help your team to know where they stand.
- **Convey regular feedback.** Be sincere and criticize fairly. Give feedback promptly about things that go well and about things that go awry. Always one on one, never in front of third parties, especially not negative feedback or criticism. If you have to criticize, focus on the behavior, never the person behind it. That's not our place anyway.
- **Instill a no-blame culture.** Allow mistakes but make sure that they don't get too expensive. Don't rip anyone's head off for making a mistake. In my experience, mistakes indicate that the task and the expectations weren't communicated clearly enough or the employee concerned was unqualified for the task in the first place.
- **Be a role model.** You have to demonstrate all the behaviors you expect from others.
- **Provide leadership.** Leadership is an exercise in craftsmanship, not voodoo. You can learn and practice it.

- **Give daily checkups.** Give your people a daily checkup. Are they doing okay? What's on their minds?
- **Monitor overtime.** Yes, overtime is part of startup culture, but don't get carried away. Tasks have to be designed in such a way that they can actually be completed.
- **Be resolute.** Deciding — sometimes under pressure and with insufficient information — is part of leading. It's important to follow through on those decisions, and people expect it of you.
- **Be sensible in establishing rules.** Forget the commandments on stone tablets. A few rules of what's acceptable and what's not are all you need. Make these transparent and let the rest slide.

No founder should be as poorly prepared to lead as we were originally. There's no magic involved in setting at least a few guidelines on how to deal with challenging situations. Sure, an inexperienced entrepreneur's first conflict-resolution meeting is probably going to be a little awkward. But sufficient preparation and the right tools can ensure that it won't go completely off the rails, that nothing important will be forgotten, and so on. My advice to founders is to take it seriously! You have to realize the

importance of leadership, and people have to be able to easily recognize that you realize it.

After those wild early years and adding Winfried Rübesam, my codirector, to the team, I've been able to become more professional in my approach to leadership. We weren't a startup anymore, and with Winfried on board, we had our first professional manager who knew all the tools and tricks of team leadership. When Winfried signed on, a positive process began — a process of instilling professionalism in our leadership and culture that were appropriate to an enterprise of the size we had become.

In 2019 we in upper management got together and spelled out our understanding of leadership — naturally in a language and style befitting fritz and in our typical no-cap style.

leadership at fritz

clarity:
our tasks are as clear as our kola is black. that's why we ensure clarity about responsibilities, foster autonomy, and set smart goals.

being resolute:
we mean what we say. that's why we don't promise anything that we can't deliver, and we deliver what we've promised.

lifting and pushing:
fritz is only as good as the fritzes. that's why we lift our staff up and push them to constantly improve the business.

respect:
in order to receive respect, you have to give it. that's why we extend trust and appreciation to all fritzes.

transparency:
it's a long way to the black planet. that's why we communicate our route such that everyone knows where we're going, and we do it on a basis of transparency and equality.

passion:
we're not just anybody; we're fritz. that's why we don't do things just any old way, but with all the passion our hearts can muster.

celebrating:
what we achieve, we achieve together. and that's exactly how we celebrate our achievements.

Anyone who's worked for a big company is familiar with such goals. And similar sentences can probably be found in quite a few corporate mission statements. Still, the process of bringing one's values to mind, formulating them explicitly, and committing to them before your staff is important for every company. I often recall something a historian once told me: the Doge of Venice, the chief magistrate of the maritime republic until the end of the eighteenth century, had to read his oath of office out loud to his Great Council (who were the ones who elected him) once a year. It's safe to assume that both the doge and the nobles on the Great Council would have been well aware of the content of the oath without this ceremony, but that wasn't the point. It was about *commitment*, the act of publicly obligating oneself. And that was exactly the objective of our workshop on leadership. That act of reflection and introspection is so valuable that it should be repeated regularly. Even if the results might now seem banal in retrospect, the route one takes to get there is what really counts. And even though it's hard sometimes, that mission statement does indeed determine our actions at fritz.

I've found the image of a coach and captain to be helpful in my leadership role. A coach serves as a sparring partner for their own people and sticks by them. In the rare role of a captain, what matters are clear articulations.

When the time comes to resolve a conflict or to stake out the territory for a new project, that's what's required.

An authoritarian style following the motto of "Do it because I'm the boss!" is not only completely anachronistic, it also wastes the potential of employees who have their own ideas and motivations, it frustrates employees who are committed and are experts in their fields, and it will eventually damage the authority on which it rests. And a leader who lacks the confidence to submit their point of view to questioning and criticism should ask themselves whether they believe their own reasons. I, for one, am happy that a good portion of our people ask questions, expect explanations, and consider reasons. Once, when I was asked how employees can impress me, I answered: with a steadfast, well-presented opinion. And I added, "But first I have to learn not to see it as a distraction." I have since learned that I need to create a space where others can flourish and ask critical questions. That's why I am never the first to speak at internal meetings; others might interpret that as "the boss setting the boundaries." And I try to express myself with questions more than statements. As important as it is to lead and make space for necessary dialog, it also has to lead to a result and a decision at some point. And it's not necessarily me who decides. It can also be the person with

the greatest expertise on the question at hand, man or woman.

Of course, the ability to make decisions doesn't guarantee that all those decisions will be the right ones. I usually reach decisions quite quickly, sometimes straight from the hip on the basis of my experience, and then I communicate the result clearly. But I can also admit it if my decisions turn out to be wrong. If the boss suddenly pulls a 180 or makes a mistake, it's very important to discuss it openly. Something like "Sorry, folks, I misjudged the situation, and I would decide differently today" is the minimum. A leader who cannot admit their own mistakes betrays their own insecurity. That's not the way for a captain to inspire loyalty.

The most important thing when switching back and forth between the roles of coach and captain is to keep in mind which role you're performing at any given moment. And what do others (justifiably) expect of me? A boss who suddenly mutates from the understanding listener to the authoritarian decider in the middle of a meeting would throw any employee off balance.

Difficult meetings, ranging from serious personal conflicts to reprimands and terminations, are also a skill that must be learned. In my opinion, three things are key: good preparation, empathy, and clarity. You can't stumble into a meeting like that on the spur of the moment (especially not when you're still angry) without knowing what should come of it. You have to be able to imagine what the other party is going through. And you can't let fear of emotional reactions garble the message so badly that the message you wanted to communicate isn't understood with crystal clarity afterwards. My experience with communication in difficult situations is that most employees, men and women alike, prefer clear messaging, especially in times of crisis.

fritz has had to continually reorganize and assess which tasks have become superfluous and which should be redelegated. We're tuning the vehicle while moving at full speed and full capacity.

One thing I've learned in my time as an entrepreneur is that it doesn't really matter to me where, when, and how our staff complete their tasks. I don't really care if someone is an "at-the-last-minute" personality who chills until Thursday morning before getting started on their weekly targets as long as they get the job done on time and as well as expected. I had to learn that too. I used to fret much more about people stopping for a chat, leaving early, coming in late, or working from home. Now I abide by the wisdom that "we've rented their heads, not their asses."

After years as a lone wolf, I had to learn in those early years that it's the employees that make a company. I have since grasped that an entrepreneur's most important task is to take care of their people and to assemble the right team. It's a complex, multifaceted, and incredibly energizing task even when things are going smoothly. Not taking it seriously is probably one of the biggest mistakes you can make.

The competition likes to approach fritzes anyway. It's common knowledge in the industry that we are quick to give employees responsibilities of their own, that they achieve solid results at a rapid pace, and that they're team players. fritz looks good on a resumé. And when people go in the opposite direction, coming to us from the major corporations, they appreciate the short distance between proposal and decision and the autonomy we grant our staff.

As the ownership structure was changing, many fritzes were nervous, especially during the interval when it was clear to everyone that something was amiss, but we weren't yet able to go public with the impending change. That inspired our competition to launch targeted poaching attacks aimed at our best people, and our turnover increased notably.

Now, nearly five years later, we have been certified as

an "Attractive Employer." This certificate is awarded by an independent institute following a survey of the company's employees, and it's the result of hard work, greater professionalization through workshops, new ideas brought in by fritzes joining the company from outside, and talking, talking, talking. Our corporate culture is certainly one reason that people feel so comfortable at fritz.

I'd like to give you a peek inside out corporate culture using the iceberg model. The visible part of the iceberg corresponds to the goal, the strategy to achieve, and the image projected outward. I've already described one part of our goal above in the section on purpose. In simple terms, the strategy can be defined here as "continuing to grow with good customers in hospitality and retail along with our fans." The image we project outwards in a mono-chrome, urban, contemporary style with hoodies and sneakers reflects it well. That's how many people know us. The invisible part of our culture, which corresponds to the submerged portion of the iceberg, includes our rules, our rapport, our values, and our mentality. To illustrate, let me share a few little episodes from our recent past.

Sometimes things creep slowly into a corporate culture, even though they don't really match the company's values at all. fritz ran into this problem when it

came to company cars. As our startling growth and solid performance reduced the need for frugality, we assembled a huge fleet of vehicles prior to 2017. Even fritzes who hardly left the office and could easily commute by bike or public transport would come to work in a company car. At some point, our sales reps had transitioned from utilitarian VW Golfs to SUV road tanks, which were too heavy, too big, consumed too much fuel, and emitted too much pollution. They were like the Great Pyramids on wheels: big and imposing on the outside, musty and antiquated on the inside. It was a gradual process that continued until we cleaned house. We developed transportation guidelines, returned our leased leviathans, chose smaller, more economical models for all our new sales reps' vehicles, and created incentives for our staff to commute by bike or public transport. We moved our offices to a more central location that was easier to reach without a car, we offered fritzes transit passes for public transport or a job bike. Our sales reps started driving ever smaller cars and some of the first electric vehicles. And we tested using bikes for our sales reps in some markets, like Berlin and Hamburg. Sales reps, of course, need vehicles to do their job, but we can't go around preaching sustainability and promoting reusable glass bottles while sending our people out into the world driving gigantic gas-guzzlers.

These changes weren't easy for everyone to swallow. It's surprising how many people associate cars not only with comfort, but also with prestige, status, and personality — even today. But for the most part, the process of decommissioning our fleet, at least its biggest battleships, has resonated positively.

Sometimes a single moment in the bustle of everyday business is all it takes to discover where you're falling short, perhaps only in terms of your own values, and to initiate a change. One time, late in the evening, I had to go fetch something from an old, low-ceilinged warehouse where we kept promotional materials. When I flipped the light switch, rows of neon lights illuminated one after the other. Before me I saw piles of chalkboards packed in plastic foil, sandwich boards, ice buckets, necklaces, t-shirts, straws, and a landslide of soon-to-be plastic garbage. Customers tend to use these materials only briefly, perhaps for a few days or weeks, before chucking them in the trash. And then they go straight into the incinerator. Ouch! It hurt. Supplying the landfills is not what I had in mind as an entrepreneur. That experience was a few years back, and since then we've been able to almost eliminate our plastic consumption. To reduce the number of promotional items, we've completely eliminated our disposable swag and we've switched to

sustainable materials like paper and wood, where possible. Advertising products is just a matter of course for many restaurateurs and supermarkets, but we (and others) can now offer promotional materials that are either largely recyclable or that are decorative and durable enough for our customers to use for a long time.

Symbols matter, and it was the right move for us to resolve the obvious contradiction between our words and our deeds.

take a stand! our philosophy

We live in such interesting times that I cannot imagine failing to take a stance on social and political issues. And that goes not just for me personally, but also for the company that I cofounded and continue to represent to the world. Entrepreneurs bear a responsibility, and they are one of society's many pillars; they can help to tear it apart or to build it up. Let me mention just one of many examples: Antje von Dewitz, the entrepreneur behind VAUDE outdoor equipment. Along with other, like-minded entrepreneurs, she started a program called "Right of Residence Through Work" (*Bleiberecht für Arbeit*), which works to help integrate refugees.

As the entrepreneur behind fritz-kola, my team and I are facing growing responsibilities to work toward a more sustainable and democratic society. Maybe it's easier for us to make a contribution with a modern kola than it is for other companies. But other entrepreneurial families have also accomplished remarkable things. For example, the family behind Vorwerk, known for its household appliances among other things, launched a campaign in 2019 that contained a statement that seems self-evident, but that gains significance in a time marked by a rising radical right party promoting a jingoistic platform: "There's a reason the label says *Made in Germany*, not *Made by Germans*." The special labels that we developed for the 2019 Human Rights Film Festival in Berlin and pasted onto every second bottle in circulation made a similar point. They depicted two hands holding each other and read "All people are equal — everywhere." This message supporting the tolerance and human rights that inspired the festival applies just as much to us.

Perhaps the founders behind the Ben & Jerry's brand of ice cream have inspired me subconsciously. Those two friends, Ben Cohen and Jerry Greenfield, released a variety of ice cream, for instance, promoting gay marriage. And when negotiating their company's takeover, they managed to get Unilever to donate

$15 million to charities of the two founders' choosing. The money went to movements like "Occupy," among others. The two founders wanted to take a clear stand.

But is it really a kola's job to engage in controversies and to publicize its stances on issues like climate change and an open, liberal society? We regularly encounter statements in the comments sections of our social-media channels calling for us to just sell our kola and keep our mouths shut. We couldn't disagree more, and we take a stand on issues that are important to us. After all, a company is made of people, people with opinions and stances.

Our society is facing a number of challenges:

- **Global warming:** At the 2015 United Nations Climate Change Conference, 163 countries agreed, within the context of the United Nations Framework Convention on Climate Change (UNFCCC), to keep man-made climate change well below 2°C compared to the pre-industrial era. Keeping it under 1.5°C would be better. That's why we're currently working on paying that bill and going climate neutral. It's not easy, but the numerous measures described in this book show that we're on the right track.
- **Local society:** How can we make a positive contribution with our business to the local society where we

operate? Can we add value locally by hiring and
paying our taxes locally?

- **Liberalism and democracy:** Liberal and open societies
are having a rough time at the moment in the face of
rising populism and exclusion. How can we counter
these trends and advocate a liberal, democratic
society? Are we doing enough, and are we doing the
right thing? Time will tell.

The billboards we ran during the G20 summit in the
summer 2017 in Hamburg, which bore the slogan "Wake
up, man!" were one of our most famous campaigns. The
goal we wanted to achieve with that campaign was to
inspire the local population to take a stand and to
participate in the debates happening around and about
the summit. We doubted whether the summit was really
going to make any progress on issues like intercultural
understanding, fighting climate change, and a more just
distribution of wealth.

It became increasingly clear in the months leading up
to the event that the meeting of heads of state and
government was going to cripple the city and cause plenty
of political turmoil because the mainstream attitude in
Hamburg is decidedly open and liberal. Tragically, the
extremely imaginative forms of protest performed by a

large number of peaceful demonstrators were overshadowed in the public perception by images of burning barricades and businesses.

We had thought in advance about how we would react to the summit. We eventually came up with the idea of the sleeping politicians as a contrast to our call to wake up and do everything possible for a better world of democracy, environmental conservation, and social justice. The only question was to decide which three politicians we would depict sleeping soundly like busted criminals. Trump and Putin were givens; Erdogan also passed the test. Our brief to the ad agency and the artist Sutosuto stated: high-quality art, no caricatures, not disparaging.

Many were grateful to us for this statement in the name of the summit's opponents.

One social project that has always appealed to us is called "Every Bottle Helps" (*Pfand Gehört Daneben*). This program, founded by Matthias Seeba-Gomilla, has raised consumer awareness about not putting reusable deposit bottles into the trash. It's a familiar sight: a nice, warm day, crowds fill the parks and plazas, and people buy a soft drink, kola, or beer in the stands and kiosks nearby to enjoy with friends while hanging out. Around 180 million euros land in the trash each year because people just

drop their deposit bottles into the next garbage can rather than returning them. The "Every Bottle Helps" program reminds everyone to put their deposit bottles neatly next to the garbage cans. Doing so saves those who depend on returning those containers for the deposit the trouble, danger, and indignity of digging through the waste bins. Moreover, it ensures that far more of these reusable bottles make it back to be washed and refilled at the bottling plants rather than in the garbage incinerators.

The program dissolved in 2015 because Matthias had to give it up for lack of time. We were asked whether we'd like to keep it going. We figured, why not? It fits our social and environmental values perfectly. Passionate fritzes have been investing lots of time and effort into the program ever since to convince as many producers as possible who use reusable deposit bottles to participate in the project. Their commitment is what allows us to support "Heat Help" during especially hot periods. This is a program in which we call on organizations like GoBanyo and the Karuna social cooperative to distribute water bottles to the urban homeless. Train stations are where their success is most visible, when perfect strangers pass sealed water bottles to the homeless and go on their way with a wave.

As of 2020 we have been able to convince over 80 partners to join the "Every Bottle Helps" program, many of whom are also beverage producers interested in helping the needy to tap bottle deposits for an income. Rebranded as "Every Bottle Helps," we've also started to export the program into the Netherlands and Poland. The initial steps are especially challenging in those markets because deposits on bottles are not as widespread as they are in Germany, so we first have to educate people about the principle behind it.

People often ask me how much space is available within our company for political statements, how much is there for those we make to the outside world, and how do we find a reasonable balance.

We have an advantage over other businesses in this respect because we've been transparent about our stances from the very beginning. Anyone who comes to us knows exactly what they're getting. Anyone who's allergic to our cultural DNA at fritz isn't going to apply here anyway. Taking a public stance and being transparent about your beliefs is something you have to want as a brand and as a company. It has to fit, and everyone has to get behind it and feel comfortable with the stance taken. Dealing with the inevitable criticism internally and from the outside, possibly including

strikes and boycotts, is a part of it that you simply have to accept.

In 2016 the newspaper *Die Welt* asked me whether fritz is the more politically correct kola. My answer expresses the ambivalence common to any classic business that is trying to take a stance while simultaneously making a profit: "Buying from domestic producers is certainly good for the local economy. Four [now five] bottling plants work for us, producing locally in Germany. We don't have any subsidiaries that abscond to tax havens with our profits. We pay all our taxes. That's actually a positive nowadays, being a company that pays for the infrastructure, education, and the social atmosphere that benefit us. So yes, as far as that goes. But at the end of the day, we're just a normal, private company competing in the market."

Combining business interests with a social conscience can be controversial. When a film about the G20 protests that we had sponsored was screened in the Abaton cinema in Hamburg, I was on the podium with generally more leftist-alternative speakers, and I was introduced as a representative of "small-c conservatives." I received criticism for our billboard campaign with the sleeping politicians because our political statement was virtually inseparable from its commercial purposes. My answer:

sure, we have to earn money. And yes, we take a stance. And again yes, hermetic separation between the two is impossible. We use our privilege to communicate our message. And the stances we take are, of course, useful in that they reinforce our fans' identification with our product. I can put an even finer point on it: as an entrepreneur and a merchant, one very important reason I'm against war and racism is because they disrupt the stability I need to conduct business. But people always come before profits.

I can understand that combining a political position with the pursuit of profit leaves a bad taste in some mouths. But I really don't find it problematic. It would only be dubious if our stance weren't authentic, but only a marketing ploy. But that's not the case. Our former marketing guy, Patrick Keller, put it like this, "fritz-kola isn't just an alternative business, and it's not just a commercial success story; it's both, and not both in equal proportion, but 100 percent both."

founding with a friend?

One of the questions I'm most commonly asked is whether it's a good idea to found a company with a friend. Wouldn't it be better to cleanly separate friendship and business? This question naturally came up after Lorenz left the company in 2016. I know that many people clearly sever those two areas so that they don't lose both — the friendship and the business — if things go south. An acquaintance's parents repeatedly turned down a friend's very lucrative job offer, saying "We want to keep you as a friend, and we don't want to jeopardize that friendship with a business relationship."

I still don't consider it a mistake to have gone into business with my then best friend Lorenz. In light of our success, the very idea is absurd. We were the perfect team in the founding stage back in 2002. We had been very close friends ever since our Scout days. We didn't exactly live together as students, but we hung out together constantly. We had the same taste in music. We even took a trans-European rail tour together in 1998. The best of friends. Our outlooks were similar, and we complemented each other well. We had similar attitudes, goals, and preferences. We usually managed to keep our gaze focused on the business, and we rarely spared each other or ourselves criticism and straight talk to preserve the friendship. Combining friendship and business won't work if you go too easy on each other.

After gaining experience over many years as independent entrepreneurs, our own individual independence became more important to each of us. We didn't need each other as much as we had initially when we were still young, clueless, and running off halfcocked. It was good for us to be together, to know each other so well, and to trust each other so deeply. It was the foundation for our shared success. Building and running a business with a buddy was exactly the right course of action for quite a while. But what does it say in the Bible? "For everything there is a season …"

There's also another way to look at it. Considering the challenge and responsibility that founding a business represents, it's a miracle that the two-friends-become-entrepreneurs plan actually worked as long as it did in light of all the biographical and commercial ups and downs over fritz's first 15 years.

It's like many longstanding marriages. Two people walk the same road for quite a while, and at some point, they decide that their paths are diverging because they're running out of common ground and the differences are becoming overwhelming. I feel sorry for people who look

back on many years together and can only see the negatives, even though they may have raised some great children together, shared some great experiences, and overcome numerous obstacles. Sadness and bitterness are natural at the end of such a process, but that shouldn't discount all the good times and common achievements.

Speaking of marriage, those with a more rational than romantic bent will settle the terms of the divorce right at the beginning while things are still going well. That's what Lorenz and I did too. Back in 2002 we spelled out the articles of association for our partnership, and the worst-case divorce scenario was already included. From the very beginning, we considered the possibility that we could split up someday. And when it came to pass, we adhered completely to our agreement. But for a long time it was a venture between friends, not a common business enterprise, and I still look back fondly on that.

Our distinct personalities were also a factor in the success of our business. Our friend Peter put it this way:

The combination and the positive friction made the difference. Lorenz was more blunt, brief, factual. He had the typical, direct, Hamburg way of expressing himself. A little like the sharp-tongued actor Jan Fedder, sometimes grumpy, sometimes warm, but always nice and authentic. Mirco is more of a diplomatic people pleaser. Both are very ambitious and work hard. Both had the entrepreneurial touch in how they thought and acted, but they were also grounded in the hip Hamburg scene and their clear political and social points of view.

I won't, however, sugarcoat what was a very rough situation: Lorenz leaving was the deepest crisis to hit the business until COVID. Matthias Onken, the former editor at the *MoPo* newspaper, who was like a godfather to our fritz-kola baby, was close to us at the time and later said to me: "That fritz has survived the end of your friendship without taking too much damage is probably a mix of professionalism, discipline, and luck. You managed to keep your business from going under. And you found the right investors to come on board."

The worst part was when Lorenz and I both knew that our common road had come to an end, but we didn't yet have a plan for the future that we could show to everyone else. We couldn't say anything, although many in the company had noticed that the atmosphere had been tense for a while already. In theory, I could have continued on my own, but that would have meant the business would have had to cough up all the capital required to buy out one of its cofounders. Such a buyout would have necessitated enormously high interest payments for

several years. Moreover, I, as the sole owner, would have had to rely on my own counsel at shareholders' meetings. Bringing in a cadre of competent investors was clearly the better course of action.

A bank advisor put me in touch with some consultants who had experience in trading commercial shares. Oh boy, how had I ended up here? Delivering kola to bars and cafés just yesterday, and now sitting in meetings, surrounded by people in suits and ties, in venerable old rooms with oil paintings of sinking ships on the walls. That's hilarious, I thought. Here I am planning the future of my kola, and on the walls are pictures of ships being shattered on the coast.

Fortunately, fritz-kola was doing well enough that we could afford this army of consultants. We looked at the different ways we could rearrange the company's ownership and who might be the right investors. The first new shareholder was easy to find: Dirk Lütvogt, the fifth-generation owner of the Auburg-Quelle spring water company and the central bottling plant for fritz-kola between Osnabrück and Bremen. I appreciate his down-to-earth manner, and, as might be expected, Dirk is an expert on everything related to bottling and soft drinks. Florian Rehm, from the family that owns Jägermeister, was the second investor we brought on

board. He's a branding geek in the best sense of the term, and he pummeled me with questions about brand management and global expansion. As an entrepreneur in his own right, he brings a lot of experience in international commerce and business development, which is of incalculable value when we "boldly go where no one has gone before." Or me at least.

For me, the most important thing is for fritz-kola to remain independent with this group of shareholders so that we can continue to do our thing. The only thing left was to find someone to beef up our management team. My experience reached from the garage until that point, but I simply lacked the knowledge and experience to run a company with a staff of nearly 300 on my own. At the

time, we ran fritz-kola using only two key performance indicators (KPIs): our revenue and the bank balance. You could do worse, but that's not enough for complex situations. We succeeded in luring Winfried Rübesam, a manager from the beverage industry with plenty of international experience, away from his position as CEO of Brown-Forman in Germany and the Czech Republic and to join us as CFO. Winfried and I knew each other already, having shared a few lunches where we discussed topics like branding and sales, and we shared a common past in that we had both been active Boy Scouts with a common appreciation of unspoiled nature.

Restructuring the ownership of the company in 2016/2017 pushed me to my limits physically, mentally, and financially too. Meeting with bankers, investors, and consultants every day drew my attention away from the fritzes who do the real work. Although I was able to prepare myself over a solid year for the new era of fritz-kola without Lorenz, it was like an amputation without anesthesia for many fritzes. One of the founders was suddenly gone. Nobody could anticipate what that would be like. Lorenz's departure hit many people very hard, which is one of the main reasons why it wasn't announced until I was ready to present an alternative. But my own surprise at how shaken some of the fritzes were showed me just how preoccupied I had been with the process itself.

As I now realize, we started the severance process too late, and as a result it continued far too long. Our staff thus had an even greater burden to carry. The whole thing should have been done much faster. But calling the right plays is always easier when the game is over. I advise anyone who wants to do better to come to grips with the severance as soon as possible and initiate the necessary procedures. Specifically, meet with some good advisors and set aside the time and resources to involve the staff and to cushion the blow.

25 rules that have worked for me as an entrepreneur

Here once again I summarize the basic principles that (would) have helped me in my career as an entrepreneur. Some only came to me with hindsight, and I only became able to recognize and express them after going through the experience. They aren't the last word on the subject, but for me they're a handy primer derived from my time as an entrepreneur.

personal matters

Patience and endurance. Perseverance is extremely important. Your will to achieve your goals must be unwavering. Those first years are especially tough. You're drowning in work, and you don't even know at that point whether it'll pay off in the end. In the beginning, I was living on 300–400 euros a month after rent. Some hardships must simply be endured.

Be authentic while living up to your role in the company. The trick is to balance being authentic in terms of your values and convictions, but still fulfilling your role when it comes to predictability for the team in the company. My old friends often complain that I don't have time for them anymore, but they would all affirm that I'm still the same guy I used to be.

Find a balance between trust and prudence. I've been suckered many times. Nonetheless, I've made the conscious decision to trust everyone at first, even at the risk of someone taking advantage of me. But what I gain from those who deserve the trust more than makes up for it.

Be ready for lots-n-lots of work. There will always be a mountain of work to do, even when things are going well.

Find a coach! Nobody is perfect, and nobody can do it alone. You need to know yourself well to avoid collapsing or flipping out in stressful situations, and the best way is with the help of a good coach.

strategy
Count the pennies. We wanted to avoid debt by any means possible, leaving us only with the money to spend that we had already earned. Doing so allowed us to remain independent, but it also meant that sticking our heads in the sand when we couldn't pay a bill was not an option. When cash is tight, take the initiative and call all your business partners. Curling up and playing dead isn't smart.

Keep an eye on the four Ps of marketing. Knowing how you are going to address product, price, place, and promotion is essential to your success. Is what I'm doing out there really relevant?

Don't delegate your identity. The last word on the brand, its management, and its development belongs in house, not in an outside agency.

the market

Don't compromise on quality. Can I really bring this to market? Would I want to give or receive this as a gift? Does it compel customers in its current state? You can't undo the launch of a deficient product.

Get out there. You should regularly go out where your customers are. It's easy to lose contact with the only relevant context — the market — inside your office bubble.

Spotless presentation. No matter how casual the corporate style, staff should always be immaculate and organized when encountering customers. That applies to clothes, hair, cars, documents, and so on. It's about respect, but it's also about trustworthiness. If those are lacking, the revenues will be too.

corporate culture and leadership

Set clear rules. And then follow them yourself.

Get organized. Determine procedures and responsibilities early and clearly. Chaos might have a certain charm, but it's annoying and expensive.

See the opportunity in criticism and crises. A headwind will make you work harder and eventually take you farther than a tailwind. Criticism and crises are more valuable than praise. A corollary of that is to make sure you create spaces where people can air their grievances. Figure out the reasons for the problems identified in exit interviews, if not sooner. And never punish the bearers of bad news.

Focus on opportunities, not obstacles. Try to look at things pragmatically. Where there's a will, there's a way … somewhere.

Don't dominate the discussion. Give others the floor and space in discussions and meetings.

Get everyone on the same page. Communicate, communicate, communicate. It's as necessary as it is exhausting.

Listen. Decide. Listen more. Take all good arguments seriously and give them due consideration, and then have the courage to decide without cowering in a foxhole afterwards. Correcting a mistake with good reason is better than stubbornly clinging to it out of principle.

Take difficult steps quickly. As soon as you recognize that a momentous decision must be taken, act swiftly and decisively. Long periods of uncertainty cause unnecessary damage, improve nothing, and usually make things worse. In the case of sudden or unsettling changes, staff need to be appropriately informed while it's happening and consoled and reassured afterwards.

odds and ends
Archive historic documents. We didn't do this at first, nor did we take it seriously, which I now regret greatly. Even if it's hard to imagine at first, one day you'll want that original commercial license, that first business plan, the first prototypes, the first ads, the first contract, and so on hanging on the wall in your headquarters.

React quickly to shitstorms. When trouble is brewing on the internet, speed is everything. React quickly with clear, understandable, and — of course — verifiable statements. It doesn't matter if it happens at seven p. m. on a Friday; Monday morning will be too late.

Don't lose touch. Regular input from outside about the product and communication about it ("the average-Joe test") helps to avoid misunderstandings, mistakes, and embarrassments.

Stay out of court. Your day is only 12 hours long, and going to court consumes a lot of energy, attention, nerves, time, and money. Is having the last word really worth it? But I still struggle sometimes to live by the saying "sticks and stones …"

Taxes are cool. Many don't realize how valuable and how expensive tax-financed infrastructure really is. Businesses rely on that infrastructure and profit greatly from it, so they should also do their part.

Take a stand: We live in such interesting times that I cannot imagine failing to take a stand on social issues and expressing them with the help of my platform as an entrepreneur. But beware: the path of integrity is steep and rocky.

afterword

I was just finishing up the first draft of this manuscript in February 2020, and I wanted to take my second nice, long vacation in 20 years. I knew that fritz would be in good hands during my absence. But as it turned out, the pandemic situation became internationally (and soon nationally) critical two days before my departure. We needed all hands on deck — the captain's too. Until then, I felt sure that fritz would never again be so direly challenged as when Lorenz left and we restructured the company's ownership. But we were drifting into even rougher seas. As a business that earned a significant portion of its income from hospitality and events like festivals, we had to act quickly and decisively to avoid running aground. Since March 2020, we have lost millions in revenue that we will never see again.

As soon as the entire hospitality industry was shut down, we lost fully 80 percent of our revenue literally overnight in the initial paralysis. The compulsory closure of restaurants and bars also meant that beverage distributors ceased ordering. Some even asked to return their inventories, which we had to decline. (When the hospitality industry came back to life, it took another two weeks before the inventories in their coolers and warehouses were exhausted and the orders started to trickle in once again.)

Sales continued in retail outlets, but the hoarding behavior targeted water, toilet paper, and imperishable foodstuffs instead. The supermarkets and their supply chains were so busy filling that demand that nobody had time to concern themselves with kola, soft drinks, and spritzers. The shelves were left empty, and reorders didn't come for days. On top of that, there wasn't any shipping to be had because the beverage delivery trucks were only being loaded with "survival goods," like bottled water. After a while, when we realized that the supermarket clerks were devoting all their time to essentials like toilet paper, flour, sugar, noodles, and the like, leaving them with no time to reorder and stock soft drinks, we managed to convince some of our people to come back to work on a full-time basis, to go into the stores in spite of the risk of infection, and to fill the shelves with fritz-kola. Adding insult to injury, nearly all of our revenue from staff canteens and cafeterias in factories and offices collapsed because virtually all office work was being done remotely.

Exports also ground to a complete halt. Although we have enough traction in the German-speaking countries to have customers ask for the brand by name in supermarkets, our sales in the rest of Europe are basically restricted to bars, cafés, and restaurants … all of which were now closed virtually worldwide. All those lovely places where people get

together, have a good time, and maybe enjoy a fritz-kola were shut down. Some of our local partners were hit so hard that it will take a long time until they regain the kind of business they had before the crisis.

In March 2020, we reacted immediately and drastically due to the uncertain situation. We put practically the entire staff on a government-sponsored paid furlough. Only a small crisis team remained active to process whatever orders did come in, answer the phones, and deal with the mail. Seeing the abandoned desks in the empty offices, without having any idea when things would be back to normal, was pretty spooky. In the months leading up to the crisis, we had fortunately implemented enough tools for remote work that we could reach everyone at fritz-kola via video conferences. Using #getthroughthistogether as a hashtag, we met regularly in virtual rooms to inform the team about what steps were to come and to reassure them that we would make it through the crisis as a team.

Thanks to the subsidized furloughs, the government took on our biggest expense: wages and non-wage labor costs. The willingness and ability of our functioning social-welfare state and widespread solidarity in society are what allowed companies like ours to avoid bankruptcy and layoffs en masse, for which we are most grateful. We as a society may have to pay those costs back with higher taxes after the crisis, but at least we and the jobs will still be around.

The other fixed costs at fritz were negligible since we don't produce in house. We're talking mostly overheads like rent, electricity, and so on. The bottlers have the highest fixed costs, and they've suffered terribly. We're even more concerned about our partners in the hospitality and event industries, which are among those hardest hit by the COVID crisis. And we mustn't forget our staff. They were stuck just sitting at home, and they had to manage their lives on less money than before.

Those subsidized furloughs allowed us to keep our remaining fixed costs at a level that we could service from our residual revenue. But that only worked because we cut all our variable budgets down to the quick. Our strategy was to reach out to everyone and pay any open invoices, but to delay any further expenditure until we had some idea how things were going to develop. But we told everyone to expect us to return to business as usual as soon as possible, even though nobody could tell at the beginning of the pandemic when that might be. We were hunkering down to weather a long, hard time.

From May 2020 revenues gradually started to return. People were resigning themselves to the fact that they'd be

home for quite a while, then summer came, and they wanted to treat themselves. fritz beverages started doing well even in neighborhoods that had never really produced any retail revenue. We realized that it wouldn't always be as bad as it was at first, and we were ready to risk spending a little money on small, symbolic sponsorships. Along with the Budnikowsky chain of drugstores and the FC St. Pauli soccer club, for example, we sold "Club Saver" and "Festival Saver" tshirts and passed the proceeds on to our distressed partners.

In the summer the restaurant business started to bounce back as well. After the long period of isolation, which is contrary to most people's nature, many were desperate for human contact and a good time, so they went out. We didn't even notice the usual slump in August because so many people were spending their vacation in Germany. Over the summer, we brought nearly all of our employees back from furlough.

Unfortunately, the second wave began in the fall of 2020, with the third wave in the spring of 2021 following close on its heels. Its effects were still impossible to determine as this manuscript was being finalized. Many fritzes were on reduced hours or shifts over the winter. It wasn't until the first warm days in March that we were able to get everyone back on full time.

I'm counting on the fact that the revenue we make from the hospitality industry will regain, if not surpass, its former levels in the long term. People are still going to want to hang out with others in cafés, clubs, and restaurants or maybe go to a festival, perhaps even more keenly than they did before. Having had to go without social contact reminded many people of its true value.

Remote work is going to play a bigger role than before. fritz fans are going to be increasingly buying their favorite beverage at a retail outlet or having it delivered to their homes. And the COVID crisis has taught a lesson to us as a company as well as to society as a whole: remote work works. Everyone works just as hard and reliably at home as they do in the office. The quality of life and work rose at first because people didn't have to commute, freeing them to dispose of their time more flexibly. Productive time isn't spent languishing in crowded subways and traffic jams. But now, after such a long time, we're starting to see the limits of remote work. New hires are just faces on a screen, personal connections weaken over time, and many are suffering from cabin fever. It's getting harder and harder to maintain a social atmosphere and the team spirit. We hope that we will soon have tamed the pandemic enough to allow a balance between remote and on-site work, to restore real social connections and exchanges of ideas.

During the darkest days of COVID, I noticed that there were entrepreneurs even in the industries that were hit hardest who were trying to make the best of a bad situation. There were still people trying to organize outdoor events (which we sponsored a bit) or to combat the trend of shuttered and boarded-up storefronts by converting their bars into grocery stores, as Falco Wambold did with the Gloriabar. Naturally, a few events can't restore the restaurateurs' lost revenue completely, but they weren't willing to take it lying down. One of our sales reps made use of his involuntary free time to organize a drive-in theater in his region, and another set up an online beer shop. I really admire the ingenuity and fighting spirit displayed throughout this crisis by those people with entrepreneurial DNA. They look for solutions in a seemingly hopeless situation. As I always say, the test of entrepreneurial spirit is to be found on rough seas, not in safe harbors.

During the COVID crisis, I have once again become aware of how much I value the independence that I have earned by choosing the path of self-employment. I would balk against the feeling of being at the mercy of external circumstances, which is something I share with most other entrepreneurs. Despite the crisis, the team that Winfried and I lead are still masters of our own ship to a large extent, and we can continue the journey with our first-rate team.

thank you

Just like building a company, writing a book is a team effort. I'd like to take this opportunity to thank all those who have been a part of it.

A thank you goes out to all my fellow travelers, the women and men, boys and girls, who have been with fritz-kola and with me over all these years …

To my co-founder Lorenz for those first intense and beautiful years. For the unforgettable business meetings over spaghetti Bolognese. To Steffen Laube and Christian Augusta and their Berlin-Connection; a special thank you to "drive on ahead, I'll be along shortly. You just have to knock and say that Steffen sent you." For stories unforgotten and often retold: Martin Drechsler and our missions in Wendland, Juan Gravalos for his effort at the Greek place in Frankfurt, Norman Sonnenrein for being the hero without a cape come fair weather or foul, and Ulli Bächle for countless hours in southern Germany and Switzerland.

Dirk Lütvogt, our co-owner and operator from the Auburg-Quelle spring water company. He believed in fritz-kola before others had even heard of us, and he gave us access to modern production plants for the first time. Dirk

passed away suddenly while this book was being finalized. Dirk, we will miss you, your honesty, and your steadfastness.

A thanks to Dr. Oliver Thomas Domzalski for the many hours of discussion and transcription, to Silvie Horch for editing, to Ely Elisabet Scholle the tough project manager, to Katha Rehder for her covering fire, to Rocket and Wink for the book cover, to Daumenkino for all the years of their brilliant design, to Rebea, Sascha, Jana, Patrick, Falco, Gerrit, Himmy, Thorsten, Matthias, Peter, Joachim, Lars, Flow, and Azadeh for all your stories. Also, many thanks to Ben Kamis and the team at Fortuna Communication for the translation and the help getting this book out in English.

Thank you to all beverage distributors. We're your biggest fans.

"fritz and Goliath" describes the startup years of fritz-kola and its transformation into an increasingly European indie brand. Therefore, I owe special thanks to my European companions, like Peter and Sune in Copenhagen, Luis Figueira in Portugal, Urban Drinks with Anton and his Crew in Moscow, Claudio von Dewisa in Switzerland, Jean-Luc from IBB in France, Tarmo in Estonia, Filip in Prague, Andre in Odessa, Bas in Amsterdam, Nicolas in Brussels with Lovibond, Bruno and Ivan in Luxembourg, the Polish caffeine cartel, Del Fabro Kolarik in Vienna, Morandel in western Austria, and Stefan von Gevos in South

Tyrol, Cirjan in Bucharest, Peter and his Drykeservice in the heart of Malmö, Ramon all over Spain, Luis in Portugal, Paul of Fourcourners in Ireland, Tiia and the Diamonds, Balázsi in wunderful Budapest, Nikos in Thessaloniki, Zvonimir in Rijeka.
It is all about people.

My greatest and final thanks go to my family and to all present and future fritzes. Thanks for now and the immense anticipation of all the years still to come. The best is yet ahead of us.

© Eva Häberle

Mirco Wolf Wiegert was born in 1975 in Hamburg. After completing his compulsory civil service and an apprenticeship at a shipping company, he attended college, majoring in foreign trade and international management. He founded fritz-kola in 2003 together with a friend from his Boy Scout days. As the managing partner, he's the entrepreneur behind the indie brand.

List of images

Black and white images: © fritz-kola
Full-color images in the section to follow are courtesy of Mirco Wolf Wiegert and fritz-kola, except:
Pages 8 – 9, The Party: © Thomas Sprenger
Page 12, top, Drink from glass: © Pretty Good People
Page 12, bottom, the bottle-washing machine: © Florent Jalon
Page 13, bottom, the G20 summit: © Thomas Sprenger
Page 14, bottom, Hafendieb: © Christian Perl
Page 15, top, with Kathi and Winfried: © Maurice Rieger

with the scouts in sweden

one of our first customers, the "gloriabar" in hamburg-eimsbüttel

my second vw van after the first one broke down. the decal on the front
was already on it when i bought it from some other students

the office in loksteder steindamm with anna, britta, and norman

at a gastronomy trade show. we made and glued everything for the booth ourselves:
banner, mirror, refrigerator ...

one of our first customers in berlin, "café wahrhaft nahrhaft", here when it was still in the mtv building (franziska gebert, betty muschen)

my father visits me at the internorga beverage fair

one of our first promotional items. we bought the lamp at ikea, hand-applied the stickers, and then delivered them to the bars. cheap and available in small quantities

tanja schuster at the warehouse olympics

our very first warehouse, with the vw golf we had bought in installments parked in front of the building

anjola, after the successful relaunch

the octopus on dock 11 in hamburg harbor

with steffen laube, our first man in berlin

the poster after we had pledged to no longer dump the red & white cola

me on my way south to our austrian bottler

our first customers in great britain, florian and azadeh

the banner across from the "rote flora" in hamburg's schanzenviertel district

our protest
against the flood
of plastic bottles

a crashed truck
on the way to the
bottling plant

our bottles
before going
through the
bottle-washing
machine

speed for kids who go to waldorf schools

our "hey man, wake up!" campaign at the g20 summit in hamburg

an initiative against xenophobia by mid-sized german companies

the "every bottle helps" campaign in
cooperation with hafendieb

for a change in perspective and more
human dignity

with kathi (brand manager) and winfried rübesam (co-director)

in chemnitz at a demonstration against right-wing extremism

werde clubretter:in.

pandemic aid in collaboration with the st. pauli soccer club and clubkombinat

the fritz leadership team: second row, from left to right: lukas steinberg, valerie karbowski, marlene vaick, winfried rübesam, philipp beindorff, ivonne anton, lars schlatermund, oliver moritz, folke dienstbir, oliver heimburger, mathis weber, stefan menzel, björn knoop, oliver kelch, marcus groh, joachim stürken, katrin bartilla, katharina weichel.
front: mirco, christoph gröne